50

5-Minute Fixes
to Improve Your Riding

Simple Solutions
for Better Position and Performance in No Time

Wendy Murdoch, creator of *Ride Like a Natural*™

Trafalgar Square
North Pomfret, Vermont

This book is dedicated to my mom. Thank you for all your love and support.

First published in 2010 by
Trafalgar Square Books
North Pomfret, Vermont 05053

Printed in China

Library of Congress Cataloging-in-Publication Data
Murdoch, Wendy.

50 5-minute fixes to improve your riding : simple solutions for better position and performance in no time / Wendy Murdoch.
    p. cm.
Includes index.
ISBN 978-1-57076-455-4
1. Horsemanship--Miscellanea. 2. Horses--Behavior--Miscellanea. I. Title. II. Title: Fifty five-minute fixes.
SF309.M845 2010
798.2'3--dc22
                    2010011273

Photos by Wendy Murdoch except: vi, 1.1, 1.2, 1.3, 6.3, 6.4, 6.5, 6.6 A & B, 11.1 A & B, 11.2 A–C, 12.1, 20.2, 20.3, 20.4, 21.1 A–C, 23.1, 23.2, 23.3, 23.4, 23.5, 24.1 A & B, 24.2 A & B, 31.1, 31.2 A–D, 32.1, 32.2, 32.3, 32.4, 32.5, 32.6, 34.2, 34.3, 34.4, 36.1 A & B, 36.2, 41.1, 41.2, 41.3, 46.4 A–C, 47.2, 47.3 A & B, 47.4 A & B, 47.5 A & B (Elizabeth Rouse); 9.1, 9.2, 9.3, 9.4, 9.5, 9.6, 12.2, 12.3, 12.4, 12.5, 13.2, 13.3, 13.4, 13.5, 17.1, 17.2, 17.3, 17.4, 25.1, 25.2, 25.3, 25.4, 26.1, 26.2, 26.3, 26.4, 27.1, 27.2, 27.3, 27.4 A & B, 27.5 A & B, 27.6, 27.7, 45.7, 45.8 A & B, 49.1, 49.3 (Joyce Harman); 29.2 A–C (Pam Woolley); 45.1, 45.2, 45.3, 45.4, 45.5, 45.6 (Bradley Schneider)

Illustrations by Katherine Brown-Wing

Book design by Carrie Fradkin
Front cover design by RM Didier
Typefaces: {ITC Century, Helvetica Neu}

10 9 8 7 6 5

Contents

About the Author

Wendy Murdoch, an internationally recognized equestrian author, instructor, and clinician for over 23 years, teaches her students how to do what great riders do naturally. Wendy's desire to understand the function of both horse and human, and her love of teaching capitalizes on the most current learning theories in order to show riders how to exceed their own expectations.

In 1984, while attaining her master's degree in equine reproductive physiology, Wendy suffered a severe riding accident. Her self-rehabilitation started a quest to understand and answer the question of how to ride pain-free, using the body as it was designed. Wendy's uncanny ability to find and study with the best people in a variety of fields and her profound curiosity make her unique.

Her studies include an apprenticeship with Sally Swift, as well as extensive training with Linda Tellington-Jones, Dr. Joyce Harman, Jon Zahourek (Anatomy in Clay®), and Dr. Hilary Clayton. To help her guide students toward better function, Wendy became a Guild Certified Feldenkrais Practitioner® and continues her study with Dr. Feldenkrais' first assistant, Mia Segal. Her fascination with the mind/body connection between horse and rider has led her to explore courses outside the equine world and bring that information to her students.

Wendy combines her creative talents with her scientific training to break down larger concepts of riding into simple, easy-to-do exercises for students of all ages, abilities, and disciplines. Her ability to make learning enjoyable, engaging, and fun through in-depth presentations—both mounted and unmounted—which are easy to comprehend, helps her students "connect the dots" and achieve their riding goals.

Wendy writes articles for a wide variety of magazines and is a regular contributor to *Eclectic Horseman Magazine*. She is the author of *Simplify Your Riding* and creator of the three-part *Ride Like a Natural* DVD series. For more information, go to www.murdochmethod.com.

Acknowledgments

Countless riders, students, and friends have helped in the creation of *50 5-Minute Fixes to Improve Your Riding: Simple Solutions for Better Performance in No Time.* I would like to thank all my students whose riding difficulties prompted me to come up with innovative solutions. Many of these solutions were impromptu, and I have since used them to help other students improve their riding. Other ideas came from a variety of sources including my education and training in the Feldenkrais Method®, Bones for Life®, TTEAM®, and my years of working with Sally Swift. It would be impossible to list the source of every idea; therefore, to all who have in some way been a part of this project, my deepest thanks.

For giving the original articles life I would like to thank Darlene Jacobson, editor of the *Virginia Horse Journal*. In 2004, Darlene asked me to write a series of short, how-to articles. Five years and more than 50 Murdoch Minutes later, these articles have been brought together in this book, published in a number of print magazines, as well as online. I would like to especially thank two publications and their readers—*The Horse's Mouth* (Patty Oxendine, Editor) and *The Salt Block Gazette*—for keeping me going when I thought I couldn't write another Minute!

Also thanks to my students who were photo models for the Murdoch Minutes. You and your horses were eager and willing to do whatever I asked without question or complaint. Pam Veach and Thunder stood like statues! Special thanks also to Elizabeth Hamilton and Howie, who in addition to being photo models were the subjects for the Video Murdoch Minutes available on my Web site and on YouTube. (Howie thought the best part was eating Emily's lunch!) Thank you also to videographer Emily Kitching of Eclectic Horseman Communications, Inc, for helping me with the video minutes.

When it came time to compile the photographs for this book, I realized I had to retake almost all of them due to my incomplete knowledge of digital cameras and resolution issues. Fortunately, I have wonderful clients, friends, and colleagues who came to my aid. Heartfelt thanks goes to Pam Woolley, Cameron Rouse, and their horses, who agreed to model without hesitation and were excellent subjects, as well as Kim Genn and Patty Werick, who handled makeup and general assistance. Also thanks to my photographers Lee Rouse (Cameron's mother)—who also taught me how to take good photos—and Dr. Joyce Harman, noted veterinarian and an incredible nature photographer, who was the "photographer of necessity" on more than one occasion.

Cleaning up the manuscript, proofing all the lessons, and understanding what I meant to say (not what I wrote) required help from someone with a skilled eye for detail and knowledge of my teaching. Thank you Mary O'Brien (and your sidekick Beth Kellner) for volunteering to read all the 5-Minute Fixes, test them out, edit the manuscript, and make copious comments in places where I needed more clarity.

I would also like to thank Trafalgar Square Books—Caroline Robbins, Martha Cook, and Rebecca Didier—for publishing this book. Your professionalism has reinstilled my faith in publishing. Loving thanks to Bradley Schneider for all that you do and for being my biggest cheerleader, and to Izzy for "helping" me type.

Finally, I would like to thank you, the reader, for your willingness and courage to try something new and thus take personal responsibility for your own education, while considering the comfort and well-being of your best friend, your horse.

Introduction

Would you like to improve your riding? Do you have some nagging bad habits that are getting in your way? Would you like to maximize your riding time? Are you tired of your instructor saying the same things to you lesson after lesson? Perhaps you ride on your own and don't have someone give you feedback? Do you sometimes wonder if you will *ever* get better? Wouldn't it be nice to have simple techniques to correct your riding position so that you are not inhibiting your horse?

In 2005 I began writing a series of articles, "Improve Your Riding in a Murdoch Minute," offering readers quick tips. Over four years and more than 50 articles later, I have compiled the "Murdoch Minutes," expanded them, and included more photographs and illustrations to create *50 5-Minute Fixes to Improve Your Riding: Simple Solutions for Better Performance in No Time.*

The lessons in *50 5-Minute Fixes to Improve Your Riding* are short and specific, targeting the most common rider problems with simple how-to exercises designed to help you become more efficient and effective. These lessons incorporate a modern understanding of how we learn so that you can actually solve your problems with minimum time and effort.

Gaps in Traditional Teaching Methods

Traditional riding instructors deal with rider-related problems in several ways. They repeat the same instructions over and over (hoping that at some point the student will magically understand); point out a problem—such as the rider's torso collapsing to one side—but without offering constructive ways to correct it; yell at the student (as if the student wasn't already trying her best); make the student drop the stirrups and ride without them (a cavalry exercise designed for men, which fails to acknowledge the lack of torso strength in most women); or put the student on a longe line without stirrups or reins (often on a horse that is not trained for this purpose or that isn't moving well enough for the rider to get the correct input).

In many cases these traditional "solutions" aren't effective because the cause of the problem goes unresolved or because the rider can't recreate what happened in the lesson on her own. To survive the punishment the rider resorts to the same poor habit patterns that were the problem in the first place—only now gripping and squeezing even more furiously. Over a long period of time, some riders may gradually improve or become exhausted enough to hit upon a new way of sitting, which may or may not be an improvement. But this "improvement" comes at what cost in time, pain, frustration, and damage to the horse's back?

A better way to improve your position is to take advantage of the way your brain learns new information and creates new patterns of movement, which then become unconscious habits. To create a new habit—for example, heels flexed down versus "jammed" against the stirrup—you need to slow down or even stop and observe what you are doing, then explore the situation from a new direction. This approach allows you to achieve the same goal—for example, stability in the saddle—with less effort. Then you can integrate the new techniques (and in this case, less pressure against your stirrups while remaining secure in the saddle) into your riding.

In my experience when you take the time to *directly address* a particular problem it goes away in minutes because you give yourself the opportunity to acknowledge what is happening and learn a new simpler way—one that is easier to do, feels better, and most importantly, is effective. Your horse will respond to your improved position, which is the best feedback you can get!

By incorporating the guidelines I outline on pp. xiv–xix, you can *learn how to learn* thereby improving your riding (or anything else you want to do) using a simple process that is fun and pain-free. You can even use these guidelines when training your horse because his brain learns in a similar way to yours. You will feel empowered by your progress and will, finally, be able to resolve your riding problems.

Current Research into the Brain and Learning

Recent discoveries in brain research and learning processes are proving that the techniques I have intuitively used to teach riding for over 23 years are the most effective for learning. Regardless of age, your brain is able to make new neurons (cells) and new neural pathways between cells that cause them to fire in specific patterns. You can learn new habits quickly when information is presented in a novel, curiosity-provoking way.

You and your brain are exceedingly capable of change brought about by thoughts, images, and actions. Given the neuroplastic nature of the brain and its ability to add or remove connections, it is just as capable of entrenching poor habits as it is in creating new, more effective ones. Repeating the same old habit over and over ingrains it more deeply, which means that the old habit is rapidly activated *with no conscious awareness*. You don't even realize you are doing it! How many times has your instructor told you your hands were unlevel when you thought they were fine?

You will continue to use an unconscious old habit until: a) you become aware of it, and b) you learn new replacement behavior. If I tell you to stop raising one hand higher than the other but you aren't aware that it is happening, how can you change it? You will become frustrated because you have no idea why your hands are unlevel or what to do to prevent it.

Instead, if I suggest you keep your hands fixed on the saddle, you have a new option. As you experiment with something other than "Raise the hand," or "Don't raise the hand," you discover why the hand was higher in the first place. You develop a new understanding, awareness, and feeling to tell you when your hands are level, thus creating a new pattern of organization in your body and ultimately a new, improved unconscious habit, which then becomes ingrained.

To create new riding habits, take advantage of the changeable nature of your brain. You need to slow down, focus calmly on what you are doing, and explore new ideas. Your brain will reorganize itself in order to succeed at the new task. In essence, you are unwiring an old habit and wiring-in a new one. This rewiring explains why old patterns can disappear in minutes.

Highway versus Byway

Your brain can quickly make new neurons and pathways, but for it to do so, you need to take a detour from your usual route. Think about driving to the barn or grocery store. The route is so familiar and requires so few brain cells, you go on "auto-pilot" and can do it "in your sleep." Now, imagine that the usual route on the highway is suddenly blocked for construction and you are detoured off the main road onto a side road. You may feel frustrated, worried you might get lost, or impatient that it is going to take more time than usual because of all the extra traffic on this road. And, when you arrive at your destination, you will likely feel a bit challenged and mentally exhausted because you had to pay attention to where you were going.

Rather than defaulting to your old familiar riding habits (your "auto-pilot"), my Fixes are designed to make you pay attention and learn new habits. This makes many of the lessons more of a *mental* rather than *physical* challenge. Some of them impose a constraint—in the example of the unlevel hands (see p. xi), this could be holding a stick under your thumbs—to prevent you from resorting to your old habit. This simulates a "Do Not Enter" sign. If you obey the constraint by keeping the stick level, you may find the real source of your problem isn't your hands. Instead, this habit may originate in your hips.

You may experience the same feelings—frustration, worry, and impatience—as in my driving analogy when you experiment with the 5-Minute Fixes. Fortunately, the horse usually responds positively to the change, which makes learning these techniques interesting and fun. If you do feel a bit irritated or impatient with yourself, that's okay. Take a deep breath and recognize that your reactions are part of the process. It means you are really getting to the heart of the matter.

Imagine driving back home on the same detour. You are no longer in a hurry. You can observe subtle details along the way because you are not fighting traffic, and you realize the scenery is quite beautiful. You are less anxious and appreciate the journey. The next day you actually look forward to the detour route even though you still have to pay attention. You discover this route is quicker—even though you are driving more slowly, you get to the barn in less time. Similarly, when you learn a more efficient way of riding you are less stressed and able to focus on other things—your horse, your instructor, and your surroundings. As you practice each Fix you will notice your overall riding improve. You and your horse will be more relaxed, which will decrease your warm-up time. It will take less mental effort to employ the new pattern, and you may even forget what your old habit was like.

Even when the main highway is no longer under repair, you continue to take the detour, but let's say that one day, in a rush, you jump on (*revert to an old riding habit*), and the next thing you know you are grabbing the wheel, holding your breath, and cursing at other drivers. Suddenly you realize how stressful this route is and how strongly you react to all the traffic. In that moment, the detour (*the new habit*) becomes the most obvious choice for getting to the barn in the future. It is not unusual to revert to old riding habits especially when you are tired, stressed, or in a hurry. This is part of learning and should be acknowledged, instead of avoided. Use the experience as an opportunity to observe what happens when you take the old route. Eventually, the route of choice will be a "no-brainer." You get in your car and take what used to be a detour without thinking about it. You can take the highway if you want, there is nothing stopping you, but you've realized the detour is actually faster, easier, less stressful, and more enjoyable. You have created a positive new habit in your brain!

As you become more familiar with the Fixes, you will gradually see an overall pattern emerge. While it might feel like each Fix has a separate destination, you'll discover that they are all heading for the same place—efficient use-of-self in your riding. This efficiency will create a sense of ease and allow you to "enjoy the scenery." You will no longer be obsessed with "remaining in control" or worried about maintaining your balance. Your new position developed through the 5-Minute Fixes will not only *feel* good, it will *look* good. Efficient movement is always graceful and elegant. From now on remember to check out the detours and enjoy the ride!

Guidelines to Learning

Here are some general guidelines to keep in mind when using any of my 50 Fixes:

- ### *Give yourself a moment to focus.*

You learn best when you are able to focus on a new task. Learning is severely impaired when you are tired, hungry, stressed, or feel unsafe. Make sure your basic needs are covered. Take a few deep breaths and let go of any unwanted thoughts crowding your riding time.

- ### *Go slowly.*

Slowing down allows you to notice what is happening. Think of going slowly as "expanding" time. For this reason, many of the Fixes begin with you off the horse; mounted and standing still; or at the walk to allow you time to pay the necessary attention required in order to form new habits. Once you know how to do what you want, you can speed things up.

- ### *Do less.*

People typically work through a problem by *trying harder*. A more intelligent way is to *do less*. Doing less increases your ability to notice differences—for example, feeling less tension in your arms when you halt your horse. This has to do with the way your nervous system perceives change (see sidebar, p. xv).

Doing less does not mean you should ride as if you are a "sack of potatoes" and only ride at the walk. It means that you should pay attention to when you start to use your *muscular strength* to accomplish a task rather than *overall muscle tone* and *good physical alignment*. The minute you begin to "'muscle" through a problem, you are no longer using yourself well. Your job is to give the horse clear signals so he can understand what you want from him. Holding your breath and pushing and shoving creates tension in both of

The Do Less Principle

The Weber–Fechner Law is a scientific law that describes human response to physical stimulus. To translate this into riding, the more effort you employ, the less sensitive you become to what is happening. For example, let's say you feel unbalanced at the canter: you are so worried about steering, stopping, running into something, or falling off that you can't feel what you are doing, which is (most likely) squeezing your buttocks as tightly as possible. You notice a change in this effort only when your horse stops—or you fall off! The muscle tension in your buttocks is going unnoticed because its sensation it is not "loud" enough for you to feel when you have so many other distractions.

To use the Do Less Principle to improve your canter, reduce your effort by going back to the trot, which is easy and not stressful. Instead of cantering "almost" canter by preparing to ask for canter but not *quite to the point* where canter *actually* happens. Now, because you have decreased the overall effort, you are able to observe that when you *think* of cantering, your previously unconscious habit of clamping your buttocks begins—before you ever canter!

You come back to the easy trot again. With new awareness, you practice the "almost" canter. Gradually you can do this without the unnecessary muscular tension because you have learned to decrease the effort and increase your sensitivity, feeling *when* you start to tighten. Next time you pick up the canter, it is obvious the moment you tense your buttocks and you can change the outcome because you know how to "let go."

you. Look for the position that allows you to use the least amount of physical strength while still accomplishing the task at hand.

- *Give yourself a break.*
After you attempt a Fix for a few minutes, stop. Rest. Your brain fatigues quickly when learning new things, so give it a break! Resting between attempts is similar to the idea of "sleeping on it" when you have difficulty making a decision. Your brain actively processes the problem while you are resting and connects seemingly unrelated ideas into a new concept. Each time you return

to the Fix you will have a clearer mental picture of how to accomplish the task at hand. Your horse also needs time to assimilate new information. Remember to give him a break once in a while, too.

- *Stop when it hurts.*

If any of the Fixes cause you discomfort, please stop! If it hurts, see if you can adapt the lesson to your level of comfort by breaking it down into smaller pieces. For starters, make sure you can do the unmounted portions of the Fix without pain before trying the mounted parts. Can you determine what is causing the pain? Perhaps you are trying too hard? If that doesn't work, skip the Fix entirely. You will progress more quickly if you listen to pain rather than ignore it and attempt to push through. Often it will go away when you acknowledge the message it is sending you.

- *Listen to yourself.*

We all have the innate ability to tell when we are in balance, when something is easier, or when the horse is going well. However, many riders don't trust themselves enough to acknowledge what they feel. Instead they overanalyze the situation, cast doubt on their senses, and want to put the responsibility for determining what is "right" or "wrong" onto someone else (usually the instructor).

In each Fix I ask you to pay attention to what you sense (see, hear) and feel (touch). No one other than you (and perhaps your horse) can tell you exactly where that "right" place is because no one else can sense or feel what you do. When you accept the responsibility to listen to yourself, you will be empowered by the knowledge that you are choosing what is best for you.

- *Be willing to experiment.*

So many riders are afraid to make a mistake. The only mistake is that you are afraid! If you only focus on trying to do something perfectly you will never understand what you are doing or how it works. Therefore, most of the Fixes are based on what I call "The Goldilocks Principle": This bed is too hard, this is too soft, but this bed is just right.

It is important to experiment—explore and contrast different positions and ideas—to determine how they affect you and your horse. Be careful not to go to extremes. Just do enough each way to notice a difference (remember the Do Less Principle, see p. xv). You are simply looking for contrast—for example, knees turned out, pinched in, or resting comfortably on the saddle. If you are really concerned about how your horse is going to react to your movements, spend more time experimenting with the unmounted portion of each lesson.

- ### *Look for the detour.*

Usually, when something is difficult, we struggle through or try to rush past the problem instead of addressing it directly. With this approach, you have to keep "pushing though" every time you ride. Instead, look for the detour (see p. xii). You might find that there is a simple solution. For example, if your feet go numb when you ride because you brace against your stirrups, pretty soon you won't be able to walk when you get out of the saddle. You could buy expensive stirrups that hinge when you brace against them, but they won't solve the problem. Pretty soon your feet will go numb in them because you are still pushing! Instead, the easy detour solution would be to let your knees bend.

- ### *Go back and forth between old and new habits.*

To freely access a new movement (habit) it is important to build a "road map" in your brain. Going back and forth between the "old place" and the "new place" maps out the route. While it may seem contradictory since most riders only want to do it "right," in the end it is extremely beneficial to purposefully do something you now want to avoid—the old habit—after you have learned something new. Experiencing the difference between the two habits creates greater distinctions in your brain. This also gets your horse's attention and helps him acknowledge you are doing something different. Pretty soon your horse will tell you which choice he likes better!

Creating a "road map" empowers you because it allows you to choose what you want to do. In times of stress—at a horse show, for example—you may revert to old riding habits without a "map" to get home because the environment is different. Rather than berate yourself for being a failure, take a moment to embrace the experience. Observe what you and your horse are doing. Then imagine what the "new place" felt like. When you let go of the negative emotions you may find markers that help you get back home.

- *Use visualization and imagery.*

Visualization is a powerful learning tool. Studies show that the same areas of the brain (mirror neurons that affect the motor cortex) are active whether you participate in, see, or visualize an activity. When you visualize the activity, it is as if you are doing it! Add as much detail as possible to clarify the action. Then when you actually perform the task compare it to your visualization and see where you can flesh out the image. Remember to be careful what you watch because you can pick up "bad" images as easily as "good" ones.

- *Novelty enhances learning.*

Like brushing your teeth with your non-dominant hand, doing something in a new and different way gets your brain's attention. That's why many of the Fixes involve a variety of approaches and use different rider Training Aids to solve similar problems (for a complete list of these, see p. 198). When you add variety, your brain pays attention.

- *Curiosity is the key to managing fear.*

Fear and stress cause reaction, rather than action, in your mind and body. When you are fearful you judge yourself harshly, worry that you are doing something wrong, and become concerned that you might mess up your horse or get yourself hurt. At these moments you revert to your earliest riding habits. For example, I knew an adult event rider who, when stressed, reverted to the saddle seat riding position she learned in childhood.

When you are curious, you are open, interested, and "present" in the process. Therefore, I think curiosity is the opposite of fear. I don't believe the two emotions can exist at the same time. We are either frightened or curious, but not both. If you can become curious about what you are doing rather than fearful or judgmental, you will enhance your learning process.

- ***Have fun!***
Laughter is good for you and makes learning new habits easier. When you laugh, you breathe and relax. Often, the harder you try, the worse things get, so lighten up and laugh at how ridiculous you must look doing some of these Fixes.

How to Use the Fixes

The 50 Fixes are simple, easy, and effective. Each one requires only a few minutes to learn. Use them at the beginning and end of your ride as warm-up and cool-down exercises. After you master a Fix you can incorporate it into your daily riding routine. Occasionally, review the lessons you found particularly helpful. It is a good idea to read, study, and practice the unmounted portions of any lesson first, when applicable.

Riding Environment

Ride in a safe place on an experienced, quiet horse. Enclosed arenas are ideal. If possible, have a riding buddy or ground person to assist or coach you as you explore the various Fixes. Stop immediately if any of these lessons makes you or your horse anxious or frightened. Remember—safety comes first!

Training Aids

I have attempted to keep the items used for Training Aids simple, inexpensive, and readily available. (The complete list of those recommended in this book can be found on p. 198.) I keep almost all of mine in a bag and in my car so I have them with me at all times when teaching. (I never know when I might need the eye patch!) You will save time if you gather the Training Aids together in one place before you need them.

Each Fix Stands Alone

For easier reference, the Fixes are organized in seven sections by body category as follows (although you are not required to tackle them in any particular order):

Within each of these sections, the Fixes progress from the simplest ones first, to the more involved and the ones that use Training Aids and/or require an assistant. You may want to go through the book from beginning to end, or you may choose a category that most interests you, or you can simply let the book fall open to a page and experiment with that Fix on that day.

Color Coding

There is a color-coding system at the beginning of each Fix to identify particular requirements with a quick glance:

- **Purple:** Rider training aid required
- **Blue:** Unmounted exercise
- **Green:** Mounted exercise
- **Yellow:** Assistant recommended or needed
- **Orange:** Use caution
- **Red:** Stop!

SAMPLE RIDING ISSUES AND THE FIXES THAT SOLVE THEM

Issue	Fix
Rider unbalanced	10, 11, 14, 18, 23, 24, 30, 32, 45, 50
Rider pulling or pulled out of saddle by horse	21, 20, 22, 24, 25
Rider unlevel (feet, hips, shoulders)	5, 6, 7, 8, 9, 15, 28
Rein contact	24, 25, 27, 35, 36, 37, 39, 43, 45
Pain (back, knees, hips)	5, 7, 13, 29, 29, 30, 33, 37, 46, 47, 50
Heels down	12, 13, 29, 32, 46, 48, 49
Stiffness/tension	1, 2, 3, 4, 5, 17, 19, 20, 21, 22
Jumping position	2, 3, 4, 19, 27, 30, 33, 35
Trot (rising and sitting)	1, 19, 32, 40
Circles and turns	3, 21, 36, 37
Horse on forehand, won't go forward	4, 10, 13, 16, 18, 20, 30
Horse hollow	7, 11, 21, 25, 26, 32

Head and Neck

Introduction

Maintaining the balance of your head is extremely important. A balanced head position reduces the amount of muscular effort needed to stay upright and liberates other parts of your body recruited to help when your head is not in good alignment. Good head carriage allows you to focus on important things such as locating the next jump or letter in the dressage arena and gives you the appearance of a calm, focused presence when you ride. Not only is a well-balanced head and neck efficient, it gives the overall impression of a well-balanced rider. Keep the Guidelines to Learning (see p. xiv) in mind, especially when doing Fixes 3 and 5, so you don't hurt your neck.

1 Balancing Your Head

Use this 5-Minute Fix to balance your head. A well-balanced head makes it easier to look for your turns and move freely with your horse's motion.

> **Do you:**
>
> - **Have trouble looking where you are going?**
>
> - **Find your neck is tense when you ride, or stiff afterward?**
>
> - **Have difficulty sitting the trot?**

The solution may be all in your head. Here's a quick tip for finding a good comfortable head position next time you ride.

Pay attention to your head—that 10- to 15-pound bowling ball at the top of your neck. That's right, your head weighs as much as a bowling ball and you are carrying it around on top of your spine—5 to 6 feet above the ground—all the time. If your head is poorly balanced, your neck and back muscles have to work hard to keep from "dropping the ball."

Good head alignment means that you use a minimum amount of muscular effort to hold up your head, allowing the skeleton to do most of the work. When your head is well-aligned front to back, you can lengthen through your spine all the way through the top of your head, thereby countering the downward force of gravity (fig. 1.1).

1.2 The jaw is jutting forward. Notice how the rider's head is no longer balanced over her shoulders.

1.1 A good head position. The head is balanced over the spine. The neck is relaxed. The rider can lengthen upward through the spine.

1.3 The head is pulled too far back as if the rider is trying to touch the collar at the back of her shirt. This forced position causes her to stiffen her back, which creates difficulty when sitting the trot.

Poor head carriage requires more work than good head carriage. When you habitually carry the head forward or pulled back (in the horse, the equivalent of high carriage or overly tucked in) you inhibit ordinary movement such

Comparable Parts: The Head

Human

To state the obvious, your head contains your brain and most of your sensory organs: eyes, ears, nose, and mouth. You might be able to *feel* all over your body but you can't take in food through your toes. One of the major functions of the brain is to receive input regarding your balance, then make appropriate adjustments so you can stand, walk, run, and ride. This certainly requires a lot of "internal" attention.

For most of us, this balancing act goes on "behind the scenes" without our being aware of it. Our nervous system constantly monitors where we are in space and makes sure we don't succumb to gravity.

Horse

The horse's head also contains most of his sensory organs—eyes, ears, mouth, and nose—in addition to his brain. His head is about 4 percent of his overall body weight. In a 1,000-pound horse, we are talking about 40 pounds. The horse's head hangs on a neck that sticks out horizontally from the chest, which makes it much harder for him to balance than your head is for you.

To understand how much effort is required, grab a gallon of milk. Hold it horizontally away from your body at arm's length. I guarantee you aren't going to keep it there very long! Fortunately, the horse is designed to carry the weight of his head in this position, thanks to the strength of his *nuchal ligament*, which runs from the poll to the withers. It acts like the cable on a suspension bridge, passively supporting the weight of the horse's head.

as turning to look where you are going on a jumping course or dressage test (figs. 1.2 and 1.3). In addition, your inability to lengthen upward creates a heavy, downward pressure, making you more like a sack of potatoes on your horse's back than a good dance partner (see sidebar, above).

EXERCISE

On the Ground and On the Horse

To find a good position, slowly and gently turn your head side-to-side as you move it forward and back. Find the place where your head turns most freely.

How far down your spine can you sense the turning of your head? Do you notice movement only in your neck, or can you feel something happening between your shoulder blades or even lower in your spine? Is there any movement in your sternum?

Stop turning and notice that you breathe easier when your head is balanced. See if you can lengthen your neck so that your head moves slightly upward. Think of "pricking your ears" as if you were a horse.

As you lengthen through the neck, turn your head slowly again and find out if turning is easier. Do you sense or feel anything change in your seat when you lengthen your neck? If you are attentive you may feel your hips open and your seat deepen as you do this.

Whenever you feel "stuck" simply take a second to repeat this process to free your whole body.

2 Find Your "Feeling" Side

Training Aid
Eye Patch

Caution
Try wearing the eye patch on the ground first. Make sure you are comfortable wearing it over either eye before using it while riding.

Stop
Do not do this exercise on your horse if the eye patch makes you feel dizzy or disoriented. Remove it immediately if you feel uncomfortable.

Use this 5-Minute Fix to help you stop thinking and connect to the "feeling" side of your brain. Using an eye patch for short periods of time will help you develop a new awareness of yourself, your environment, and your horse.

> **Do you:**
>
> - Have trouble judging the distance to a jump?
>
> - Find it difficult to ride an accurate dressage test because you can't "see" a distance?
>
> - Find yourself thinking about what you should be doing when you are riding rather than simply doing it?
>
> - Tend to stare when you are trying too hard or learning something new?
>
> - Have difficulty feeling what your horse is doing underneath you?

Problems quickly arise when you start to over-think. Tension builds because you try to analyze what is happening, decide what you are supposed to do, or recall what happened in the past. You are no longer "present," feeling and responding to what is happening in the moment.

The solution may be found in the way you see and process information. Riding requires you to *think*—with your left brain—about what you are doing, such as learning your dressage test or jump course. Riding also requires you to *feel*—with your right brain—what the horse is doing underneath you and intuitively respond.

Visual information goes directly from your eyes to your brain through the optic nerves, which are part of your central nervous system. Your eyes provide a clue into your thinking process. Most everyone has a dominant eye—the eye that does most of the vision work. Sometimes closing this eye can help you access your intuitive, feeling side.

Elaine and the Eye Patch

I sometimes have students wear an eye patch, first sitting on an exercise ball and then on their horse. In particular, I remember Elaine, an analytical person, who always had the hardest time feeling what her horse was doing underneath her. During one of my clinics, she had a dramatic breakthrough. By wearing an eye patch over her dominant eye, Elaine was able to feel and *intuitively* use her aids, rather than try to think about when to use them.

Afterward Elaine e-mailed me and said: "To sum up: I used much less energy and accomplished more! It was illuminating to learn how many of my aids are applied through 'thinking' and what this thinking blocks and covers up."

EXERCISE

On the Ground

First, determine your dominant eye by making a triangle with the thumb and index fingers of both hands. Frame an object inside the triangle with both eyes open (figs. 2.1 A & B). Now close one eye. Does the object appear to move? Repeat, this time closing the other eye.

You are using your *dominant* eye when the object remains in the same position within the frame of your fingers. The object will "move" when you look with your *non-dominant* eye. If you are "right-eye dominant," the object remains in the middle when looking with the right eye. When you close your right eye (and look with your left) the object moves. For some people, the object moves when they look with either eye, which makes it less clear which of their eyes is the dominant one. For a clue, look in a mirror and see which eye is more forward (generally the dominant eye), and which one is more recessed (the non-dominant eye).

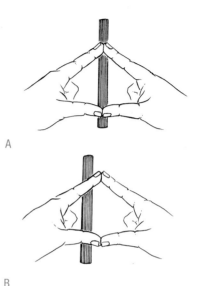

A

B

2.1 A & B   Make a triangle out of your thumbs and forefingers. With both eyes open, frame an object inside the triangle. When your non-dominant eye is closed, the object will remain centered inside the triangle (A). When you close your dominant eye, the object will move inside the triangle (B). In some cases, the object may no longer be visible.

To find out how much you habitually use your dominant eye, experiment wearing an eye patch (cheap ones are available from a drugstore or you can make your own). While in a safe, familiar environment and when able to give this exercise your full attention (not on horseback or in your car), place the eye patch over your dominant eye and wear it for a short period of time (fig. 2.2). Notice how you feel with one eye covered. Do you have difficulty orienting objects around you? Is your balance affected in any way? If you feel disoriented or uncomfortable, switch the patch to your non-dominant eye or take it off completely.

Experiment with changing the covered eye. How does each eye affect your perception of your surroundings? Slowly walk around noticing if your balance and movement change. Are you hesitant, unsteady, or stilted? Sit on an exercise ball while wearing the patch. Roll the ball forward and back observing your confidence and balance (see also Fix 16, p. 66).

On the Horse

After you are acclimated to the eye patch on the ground, experiment while riding. In a quiet place on a safe horse begin slowly, starting with the patch over your non-dominant eye. After a while, switch it to your dominant eye. Stop, and take the patch off if you feel disoriented or uncomfortable.

Notice if wearing the patch changes how you ride. Does it open up your sense of "feel"? Do you feel hesitant or timid? Do you have to find new ways of relating to your horse? Can you let go of analytical thinking? Rest frequently and remove the eye patch *before* you get tired.

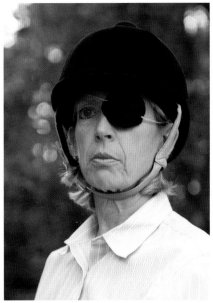

2.2 Use an eye patch to cover one eye while you ride. Change the eye patch from one eye to the other and observe the difference in your riding.

3 Look the Other Way

Caution
Be careful when looking out on the circle, especially if there are other riders in the arena.

Stop
Take a break if you feel anxious, disoriented, or dizzy.

Use this 5-Minute Fix to improve your steering. Learning to use your head and eyes independently gives you more options when riding a circle or a jump course.

> **Do you:**
>
> • **Tend to freeze up when riding?**
>
> • **Have trouble getting around a jumping course?**
>
> • **Have problems turning your horse or difficulty making accurate circles?**

Here's a quick tip to unlock your steering mechanism and get you looking where you are going.

Notice where you look: down at your horse's ears, fixed straight ahead, or always off to one side? When your horse gets startled, do you lock your head and neck in a forward position? Perhaps you've been told to look around only with your eyes but keep your head straight. Stiffening your head and neck can lead to a number of problems. It is hard for your horse to know where you want to go if you can't use your head to show him!

It is common to see riders pulling on one rein or the other to create flexion and get the horse to loosen in the neck. But we rarely consider making sure our own necks are more flexible. Of course, you wouldn't want someone pulling alternately on your ears to get you to flex in the neck, but you may want to spend a little time warming up with gentle movements.

Comparable Parts: The Neck

Human

Your head sits on top of your spine, the vertebral column. The portion that comprises the neck is made up of seven cervical vertebrae. (Your horse also has seven cervical vertebrae.)

You can feel some of your cervical vertebrae if you are careful. Start by placing the index and middle fingers of each hand behind your ears. Slowly slide your hands toward each other. Your fingers will go over two large bumps and then into a bit of a dip until they meet in the middle. Slide back to the bumps and then trace upward following a boney ridge. The ridge forms an upside down "V" or "U" at the back of your skull where your fingers meet. This is your *poll*. Take one hand and feel the length and width of your poll. From the poll, slide one finger down to the dip where your fingers met earlier. Gently raise and lower your chin while feeling for movement in this area, where the skull and first cervical vertebra, the *atlas*, meet.

Continue to slide down the middle of the neck allowing your fingers to slip into a shallow groove between the two rows of muscle on each side. Lower your chin while pressing gently but firmly to feel the hard texture of the vertebrae underneath the tissue. This part that sticks up from the body of the vertebra is the *spinous process.* Raise your chin allowing each of your fingers to search for the hardness again. You might not be able to feel all of the cervical vertebrae, especially the ones at the top, but you could possibly identify a few.

As you get to the bottom of the neck you will feel several larger bumps. Lower your head again and feel the first large bump, the seventh cervical vertebra. Just below it is another large bump that is the *spinous process* of the first thoracic vertebra. The thoracic vertebrae, which are next in line going down the spine after the cervical vertebrae, have a pair of ribs associated with them. If you continue below this point, you will feel the spinous processes of your other thoracic vertebrae.

Horse

The horse's poll is at the top of his head between his ears. The dorsal spinous processes on the horse begin with the first thoracic vertebrae. They increase in height dramatically, up to 12 inches from the third thoracic vertebra through approximately the sixth thoracic vertebra, and then gradually decline. The withers are considered the dorsal spines of the third through eleventh thoracic vertebrae (fig. 3.1).

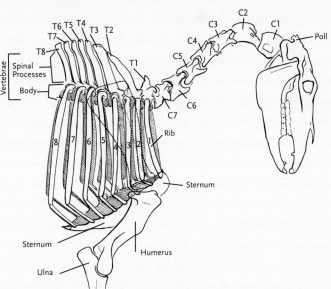

3.1 The sixth and seventh cervical vertebrae and dorsal spinous processes of the thoracic vertebrae in the horse.

EXERCISE

On the Horse

Go easy with this exercise. Only do it on a reliable mount. At first, you may feel a bit awkward or uncomfortable. If you get dizzy or nauseated, do much less or stop.

Start by walking a circle. Slowly turn your head so that you are looking out—away from the circle. When you are traveling to the right look to the left. Turn your head only as far as is comfortable. This may only be a little bit if your neck is stiff. You will know the right speed and amount if you can breathe normally as you turn your head (figs. 3.2 A–D). If you are holding your breath you are doing too much!

Slowly bring your head back to center and begin to turn it in—toward the middle of the circle. Think of your nose pointing toward where you want to look: out toward the outside of the circle, or inward toward the middle. Notice if your eyes are panning across the scenery like a movie camera, or jumping from one landmark to another. Can you get your eyes to pan smoothly?

Change direction on the circle and find out if it is harder this way. Take note if you are changing the weight on your seat bones as you turn your head, or if you are able to keep your weight evenly on both. Does your horse want to turn with you? Can you keep him tracking on the same circle using your seat as your head turns? For variety, let your eyes stay on the line you are traveling while you turn your head. Then, keep your nose on the line as you turn your eyes.

When you are ready, pick up a trot. Again, turn your head outward and inward on the circle. Make sure that the turning speed of your head is much slower than your posting speed. Count four or five trot strides as you complete the movement of turning your head from *outward* to *straight ahead* or from *inward* to *straight ahead*.

After you have mastered this exercise at the trot, repeat it at the canter. Take several strides to complete the head or eye movement. Finally, look in the direction you want to travel. Is it easier to steer now? Is your horse following your direction more clearly?

3.2 A–D Stiffening the head and neck restricts movement of the entire body (A). On a circle to the left, look out of your circle to the right as the rider is doing here (B). Allow your peripheral vision to keep track of the circle line you are riding. Turn your head in to look to the middle of the circle or even behind you—that is, over your inside shoulder (C). Finally, look ahead on the line of your circle with a wider field of vision and ease (D).

4 Eyes in the Back of Your Head

Caution
Be careful when closing your eyes while on your horse.

Stop
Keep your eyes open when your horse is unsettled or there is anything around that might distract him.

Use this 5-Minute Fix to improve your vision, "feel" and timing.

Do you:

- **Ride with intensity and fixed eyes?**

- **Stare at jumps on the approach?**

- **Have a horse that stiffens when you ask for a transition?**

- **Have a hard time getting him to completely stop?**

Here's a quick tip to soften your eyes for a calmer focus and improve your overall body presence on the horse.

Notice if you tend to stare intensely off into space or at different spots in the arena. When you ask your horse for a transition, do you hold your breath hoping for a good one? Is your balance always a bit too far forward? Learning to let your eyes rest so that you *look* rather than *stare* can help you solve these problems.

EXERCISE

On the Ground

Start this lesson sitting on a chair or bench. Look around and become aware of your face—especially the area surrounding your eyes. Do you feel pulling or tightness around your eyes? Do you narrow your eyes to focus on specific objects? Notice if your eyebrows knit together when you concentrate (fig. 4.1 A). When you close your eyes, do you scrunch the area around them? Excessive tension in the muscles that move your eyes and the surrounding facial muscles creates tension throughout your entire body.

Close your eyes again. Soften the area around your eyes so that your eyebrows broaden, your cheeks soften and drop down a little, and the area around your eyes feels wide and open even though the lids are closed. Feel the corners of your eyes relax. Maintaining this softness, gently press with your eyelids against your eyeballs as if you want the eyes to sink back in the sockets (fig. 4.1 B). It is a very subtle movement and the pressure should be very light and gentle. If you feel a lot of tension building around your eyes and in the eyelids, you are doing too much.

Be conscious of the area around your eyes as you gently press with your eyelids. Does it feel larger and begin to encompass your eyebrows and cheeks? Open your eyes and look around. How is this different from when you first started the exercise?

Stare at something in front of you. Notice the tension in the muscles surrounding the eyes and how tight and narrow this area feels. Now, sit up a little straighter. Again, close your eyes and use your eyelids to press the eyeballs back. What happens to your balance on the chair? Do you feel yourself move forward or backward slightly? What happens when you stare at something in front of you?

Generally, people notice that pressing with the eyelids shifts their balance back in the seat; while staring shifts their balance forward. Your horse can feel this small balance shift and it can influence him to move his weight toward his forehand—or his hindquarters.

Next, with your eyes open, recreate the feeling of your eyes resting back in their sockets (fig. 4.1 C). Notice how this changes your field of vision. Sally

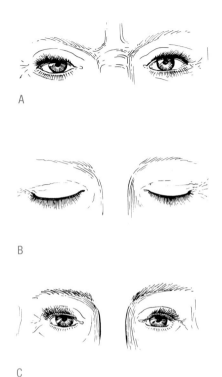

A

B

C

4.1 A–C. Intense staring eyes are shown in A. Notice the wrinkles and the tension in the face. In B the eyes are closed and the rider is using her eyelids to gently press the eyes back in the sockets. Eyes open and resting back in the sockets are depicted in C. Notice the relaxation in the area around the eyes.

Swift, in her book *Centered Riding*, called this "soft eyes." Once you are capable of maintaining your eyes gently back in the sockets while they are open, go for a ride. You can practice resting your eyes (with them open, of course) while driving in traffic.

On the Horse

At the halt, close your eyes and press with your eyelids. Feel what happens to your balance in the saddle. Open your eyes and continue to let your eyes rest in the sockets. Repeat the *resting* eyes versus *staring* eyes at the halt, walk, trot, and canter. Feel how the horse's balance changes as you switch from one to the other. Remind yourself to let your eyes settle back before asking your horse for a transition.

Lift Your Head and Chest by Opening Your Windpipe

Use this 5-Minute Fix to help better contact with your horse, improve your breathing, and give you a sense of "length" through your upper body and neck. Practicing off the horse—while driving your car, sitting in class, walking, or at work—is a good way to ensure your position in the saddle.

Do you:

- **Look down at your horse's neck when you ride?**

- **Have difficulty sitting upright in the saddle?**

- **Have trouble with your chest caving in?**

- **Quickly run out of breath?**

- **Have a neck ache after riding?**

Here's a quick tip to open the upper chest and lift your head and eyes without effort.

Next time you ride notice what happens with your head. Is it dropped forward or tilted to one side? Do you have trouble getting your horse to take the contact or lift through the shoulders? Do you look down at the jumps?

Are your shoulders rounded? Do you try to lift your chest and get your shoulders back only to find you are rigid and tense, and by the next step you have slumped again?

The tendency of most riders is to do too much or too little when it comes to solving the problem of the upper chest and head. You either pull your shoulders back strongly and/or pull your head up, or you slump and let your chest collapse down and inward. Perhaps a more anatomical image will help you find that elegant upper chest, neck, and head carriage.

EXERCISE

On the Ground

To begin, sit on a bench or chair with your feet flat on the ground. Be sure to sit toward the front of the chair with your lower legs at a right angle to your thighs (a 90-degree angle at the back of the knee). Close your eyes and concentrate on your windpipe. The windpipe is the air passageway that lies above and behind the tongue and throat and in front of the cervical (neck) vertebrae—from the back of the nose to the lungs.

As you sit quietly, think about how open your windpipe feels. Is it the same diameter all the way down or is there a crimp somewhere along the length of this "tube"? How easily can you draw a breath? How large a volume of air can you take in without effort? Does your upper chest feel open or compressed?

Breathing through your nose, drop your chin down a little and notice how this impacts the windpipe, restricting airflow into your lungs (similar to what happens with a behind-the-bit, over-bent horse). Lift your chin above its level position (similar to a high-headed horse). Feel how this position again restricts airflow. Experiment with slowly raising and lowering your chin until you find the place where the windpipe feels the most open and breathing takes the least amount of effort (figs. 5.1 A–C) Feel how much easier it is to breathe in this position. How large is the volume of air you can draw in easily?

While continuing to breathe through your nose, observe what happens to your windpipe, upper ribs, chest, and shoulders as you raise or lower your head.

Lower your chin so that you crimp the tube. Feel how the chest drops, your shoulders round slightly forward and the upper ribs barely move when you breathe. The amount of air you can take in decreases and it takes more effort for a deep breath. Raise the chin above level again and notice the effect on your breathing, upper chest, and shoulders.

Revisit the place where the windpipe is the most open and you breathe with the least amount of effort. In this position, the upper chest lifts easily, and the collarbones widen, allowing your shoulders to drop back and down. A normal breath fills your entire lungs from abdomen to upper chest, including the lungs underneath the collarbones.

On the Horse

Once in the saddle, do the same experiment with your windpipe, finding the place where it feels most open. Notice how your horse responds. Return to your old head, neck, and upper chest position. Feel what happens to your seat in the saddle and your horse's contact with the bit. When your windpipe is most open, you will be more upright in the saddle, and your horse will take a better contact with the bit.

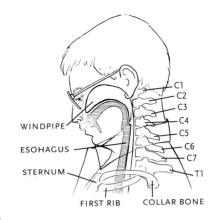

A

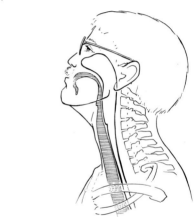

B

5.1 A–C When you drop your chin, the windpipe is restricted closer to the top end, making it harder to draw breath (A). Your upper ribs drop down and restrict the flow of air into the upper portion of your lungs. When your chin is too high, the windpipe is restricted in a different location and the chest protrudes (B). You breathe mostly in the upper chest, which makes it difficult to draw a deep breath. When the chin is level the windpipe is the most open (C). It takes the least amount of effort to draw a full breath. The air simply flows in from the vacuum effect of the diaphragm rather than you having to consciously "pull" air into your lungs.

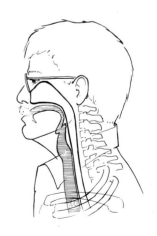

C

Chest and Upper Back

Introduction

Many riders do not understand the rib cage area of their body. They don't realize that the first pair of ribs lies just underneath their collarbones or that the free ribs at the bottom of the rib cage (the ones not attached to the sternum or breast bone) are also involved in breathing. For you to sit straight and square when riding, your ribs need to be able to move—lengthening and expanding in the front, back, and on both sides.

Rib movement is just as important for your horse. When you ask him to bend, he needs to slightly spread the ribs on the outside of the bend and close the ribs on the inside of the bend—in addition to expanding his rib cage to breathe.

Be sure to keep the Guidelines for Learning (p. xiv) in mind as you go through these Fixes. It is important to go slowly when exploring new ways to move your ribs.

6 Ribs Forward for Shoulders Back

This simple 5-Minute Fix will improve your overall confidence and balance, and help you achieve the elegant posture you desire.

> **Do you:**
>
> - Get told to "sit up straight" but can't maintain your position?
>
> - Have difficulty keeping your head up?
>
> - Feel discomfort in your upper back after riding?
>
> - Find your shoulders "round" when you are not paying attention to them?

To solve these problems most riders try to pull their shoulders back. But a much better solution is to move your upper ribs forward.

Next time you ride, notice your upper body. Do you round your upper back? Does your sternum cave in? Do you lean back to "sit up straight"? If you completely relax in the saddle, what do you do with your upper back?

The upper back is comprised of your thoracic vertebrae—the middle segment of your spine between the cervical and lumbar sections—and your

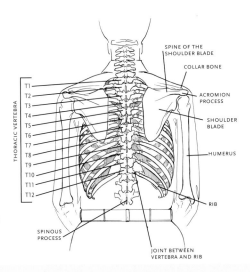

6.1   The human rib cage from the rear view. A pair of ribs attach to each thoracic vertebra.

ribs (fig. 6.1). There is a natural backward curve, called *kyphosis*, slightly rounding the upper thoracic spine. Spending long hours on the computer or driving the car can cause this curve to become exaggerated. As a result, your shoulders become more rounded and your head tends to jut forward (see Fix 1, p. 2, for a way to balance your head).

Comparable Parts: The Rib Cage

Human

Your rib cage is comprised of your sternum (breast bone) in front, 12 pairs of ribs and 12 thoracic (associated with the ribs) vertebrae. Each pair of ribs attaches to a corresponding thoracic vertebra on either side of your spine and extends forward to your sternum. There is a joint where each rib meets a vertebra on the spine, and joints where each rib meets a cartilage section connecting it to the sternum in the front (fig. 6.2 A). Therefore, the ribs are not a rigid "cage," they are moveable.

The sternum is divided into three parts: the manubrium (shaped like a Superman shield)—the uppermost segment; the body—the long part; and the xiphoid process—the end.

The collarbones (clavicles) and the first two pairs of ribs attach to the manubrium (fig. 6.2 B). The rest of the ribs are attached to the body of the sternum, with the exception of the "floating" ribs (see below). There are no ribs attached to the xiphoid process—the diaphragm and abdominal muscles attach there.

The uppermost pairs of ribs numbered 1 to 7, are known as "true" ribs because they are attached directly to the sternum through costal (pertaining to the rib) cartilage, thereby allowing them to move somewhat independently. The remaining ribs numbered 8 through 12 are known as the "false ribs." These are divided into two categories: first, pairs 8 through 10 are not directly attached to the sternum. The costal cartilage for each of these ribs joins together creating one common attachment on the sternum. Second, the last two shorter-length pairs do not attach to the sternum. Numbered 11 and 12, these ribs are known as the "floating" or "free" ribs.

continued on p. 24

continued from p. 23

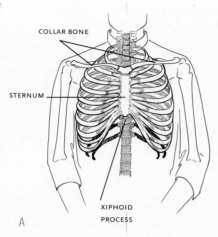

COLLAR BONE

STERNUM

XIPHOID
PROCESS

A

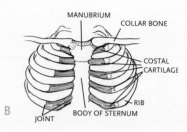

MANUBRIUM

COLLAR BONE

COSTAL
CARTILAGE

RIB

BODY OF STERNUM

JOINT

B

6.2 A–D The human rib cage from the front view (A). Ribs attach to the sternum through cartilage (B). Compare to the horse's rib cage, which has a total of 18 ribs: 8 true and 10 false (C). When you sit on the horse, you are sitting over his rib cage, as shown by these human and horse skeletons (D).

Horse

Horses have 18 thoracic vertebrae and 18 pairs of ribs. There are eight pairs of true ribs attached to the sternum and 10 pairs of false ribs (fig. 6.2 C). The sternum is very short in length, ending just behind the girth groove. The spinous processes are very tall, especially in the area of the withers. The rider sits behind the withers where the spinous processes are shorter and where they change from angling back to angling forward (fig. 6.2 D).

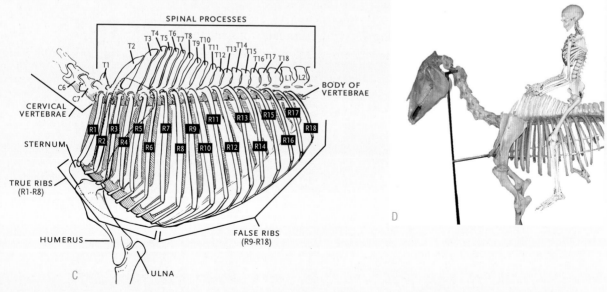

SPINAL PROCESSES

T1 T2 T3 T4 T5 T6 T7 T8 T9 T10 T11 T12 T13 T14 T15 T16 T17 T18 L1 L2

C6
C7

CERVICAL
VERTEBRAE

BODY OF
VERTEBRAE

STERNUM

TRUE RIBS
(R1-R8)

R1 R2 R3 R4 R5 R6 R7 R8 R9 R10 R11 R12 R13 R14 R15 R16 R17 R18

FALSE RIBS
(R9-R18)

HUMERUS

ULNA

C

D

EXERCISE

On the Ground

To improve your riding position, explore the movement of your thoracic spine with some help. Have an assistant gently touch your upper back in different places with fingertip pressure (fig. 6.3). The pressure should be "informative" but not painful. Feeling it through a shirt should be easy although wearing a thick jacket might interfere.

Ask her to start at the top of the thoracic spine—at the base of the neck—and touch the spinous process of each vertebra (12 in all) one at a time (see fig. 6.1, p. 23 and review the sidebar in Fix 3, p. 11). Can you feel and identify each vertebra separately as your helper's finger moves slowly down your back? Sense and feel the curve of the spine in this upper back region.

Next, have your friend rest her fingertips on one vertebra at a time. Then, with her fingers as a guide, try to move that vertebra forward and back. This will be a very small movement. The idea is to increase your awareness of the *individual* thoracic vertebra, not test the limits of your movement. At first, you might find it is easier to move only in one direction (back toward her finger or forward away from it). Continue until you have a clear image of your spine, particularly the area between your shoulder blades. Notice as you move one vertebra even a tiny bit that the overall shape of your spine changes. Rest frequently during this exercise.

Be aware of how your rib cage changes shape as you move your spine. As you round, the front of your rib cage, along with your sternum, drops and the ribs close together. As you move the spine forward, the sternum raises and the ribs open and lift. Continue making small movements until you find a place where your rib cage feels open and full in front *and* in back. Observe how your shoulders suddenly rest on top of the ribs in this position. You no longer need muscular effort to hold your shoulders in place.

On your own, collapse your rib cage in front by dropping your sternum down and move your spine back (fig. 6.4). Feel when the upper back is rounded, how the shoulders fall forward and are unsupported by the rib cage. Your head and neck will drop forward, too. Do you feel tension in your head and neck?

6.3   Have an assistant place a finger on your vertebrae, one at a time. Alternate moving the corresponding part of your back toward and away from her finger.

6.4   I have a slumped upper back. My rib cage is mostly behind my upper arm. My shoulders are rounded, narrowed, and dropped forward, therefore no longer resting on the rib cage.

6.5   I have a hollowed upper back. My back is stiff, and I have "pulled" my shoulders back. The rib cage is protruding in front of my upper arm.

6.6 A & B   A good rib cage alignment viewed from the side (A) and the front (B). Notice that my forearm hangs down vertically in line with the hip, bisecting the rib cage front to back, the shoulder blade lays flat on the rib cage, and the sternum is softly forward and up. Observe the breadth between my shoulders, the length from my neck to my shoulders, and the evenness of my left and right sides.

Next, stick your ribs out by moving your sternum and upper spine forward. The rib cage will protrude in front of your shoulder girdle (fig. 6.5). Feel the areas of tension in your neck, back, and arms. Attempting to maintain this for a period of time ultimately results in muscle fatigue and loss of position.

Find the middle ground between these two upper body positions. Notice the lack of tension in your neck and shoulders. Your head is aligned over your torso and you are able to lengthen upward through your spine (figs. 6.6 A & B). Your shoulder girdle now rests on your upper ribs, minimizing the muscular effort required to keep them back and allowing you to maintain your posture with less effort.

Whenever you hear the words "Sit up straight," or "Shoulders back," think of moving your rib cage forward to achieve a better result. (After this lesson, you might want to visit Fix 5 on p. 17. These two fixes combined with Fix 21, p. 85, will give you a good feeling of your overall upper body position.)

Head Up! Shoulders Back! Chest Out!

7

●●○●●

Use this 5-Minute Fix to discover how to move throughout your entire spine and rib cage. Learning to move the upper back will help you lift your sternum, raise your head, and widen your shoulders.

> ### Do you:
>
> - **Have trouble looking up when you ride?**
>
> - **Feel as if you can't open your chest to sit up straight?**
>
> - **Hear your instructor repeatedly tell you to get your shoulders back, but you can't maintain the position?**

Here's an exercise to help you move your upper back and open your chest.

Next time you ride, notice the distance between your collarbones. Are they close together, or wide apart? Is your head dropped forward and down, or pulled back (see Fix 6, p. 22)? Do you look at your horse's ears or at the horizon? Is your chest caved-in? Finally, can you sense and feel the upper back area between your shoulder blades? Is this area a "dead zone," meaning you have no awareness there?

The solution to rounded shoulders and looking down is found through learning to move the upper back and ribs. When the sternum sinks inward

Caution
When first resting your fists on your horse's back, be aware of his reaction. Make sure he is relaxed and standing squarely. Have someone at his head to keep him steady while you do this exercise.

Stop
If the horse drops his back or cannot stand, remove the pressure immediately. There may be too much pressure on his lower back from the saddle when you lean back. If this is the case, only do the unmounted version of this lesson.

toward the spine, your upper back rounds, causing your shoulders to drop forward and inward. Your head and neck follow the curved line of the spine formed by the upper back. In order to sit with your head up and shoulders back, you need to be able to make small but important movements in the chest and upper back. (For an explanation of the anatomy of the rib cage, see Fix 6, p. 22.)

7.1 The rider has reached back and placed her fists on the horse's lower back.

EXERCISE
On the Ground and On the Horse

First, do this lesson sitting on the floor with your legs extended in front of you, then on a quiet horse with a helper standing at his head. Pay attention and only do what is comfortable.

Lean back from your hips and place both hands behind the saddle on the horse's back. Slowly and carefully explore the horse's lower back and croup (or the floor behind you). Make soft fists with both hands and place them where you can rest on your knuckles (fig. 7.1). Be sure to keep your elbows straight. Then sit up, rest, and let your arms come forward. Repeat this process several times until you find a comfortable place for your fists and your horse gets accustomed to the position.

Again, lean back and place your fists on your horse's back. Making small movements, slowly "round" your back and return to the starting position, many times (fig. 7.2). Make sure you *fully return* to your starting position each time, pausing before you round again. Do you round only a portion of your back or do you round your entire spine from your pelvis to your head? See if you can include more of your spine each time, but do not force the movement. Sit up and rest. If you like, you can go for a walk before you continue.

7.2   Rounding (flexing) the back: Leaning back on the horse's loins, the rider rounds her back, letting her head and pelvis follow the curve.

7.3   Hollowing (extending) the back: The curve goes through the rider's entire spine, including her pelvis and head. Notice that her elbows stay straight.

7.4   The rider finds the "middle" between rounding and arching while leaning back on the horse.

7.5   The rider sits upright after the exercise. Her gaze is forward, her chest is "open," and her head and shoulders are well balanced over her rib cage.

Begin again as before, this time hollowing your back several times (fig. 7.3). Do you use your entire spine or only in part of it? Can you include more of your spine without discomfort? What happens to your head? Do you tuck or lift your chin as you hollow or do you look up? Rest for a moment, or walk around.

Place your fists on your horse's back again. Rotate your fists as if "rubbing the sleep out of your eyes." Observe how your collarbones close together and get farther apart as you rotate your fists. Arch your back as you rotate your fists one way and then the other. Does the direction your fists rotate influence how much your can arch the upper back? Again, take a short break.

Place your fists on your horse's back and this time go from starting position to *rounding* your back. Notice the difference in the direction your fists rotate. Take a break.

Once more, place your fists on the horse's back. Slowly round your back and return to start, then arch your back and return. Feel how your fists rotate if you allow the movement, so that your collarbones narrow and drop forward as you round, and widen going back as you hollow. Continue while paying attention to the area between the shoulder blades. Feel how the upper spine changes as you continue the movement.

Round and arch less and less until you find the middle between the two (fig. 7.4). Now sit upright and find this "middle place" while upright. Observe how your chest has lifted and "opened" without effort, your sight line (the level of your gaze) has changed, and your head and shoulders are more balanced over your rib cage (fig. 7.5). Ride in this middle place. Observe how your horse responds to your new sense of openness in the chest and collarbones (see Fix 5, p. 16, to find the place where the windpipe feels the most open, and combine the exercises).

Lengthen Your Sides

Use this 5-Minute Fix to improve your body symmetry. When both sides of you are more even in length, from arm-pit to waist, your weight will be more equally distributed on both seat bones. Your horse will be better able to carry you and track straighter.

Caution
Be careful when riding with one arm over your head. Bring your hand down immediately if your horse is nervous or you need two hands to steer.

Do you:

- Have unlevel shoulders?

- Hear your instructor constantly remind you to raise one shoulder more than the other?

- Collapse on one side of your rib cage?

- Feel as if you are uneven on the reins?

- Hold one hand higher than the other?

- Feel heavier on one seat bone?

- Have a slight scoliosis (curvature of the spine)?

Here's a quick tip to help you lengthen evenly through both sides of your rib cage, level your shoulders, straighten your head, and distribute your weight more evenly on your seat.

The next time you drive your car or are in front of your computer, take note how you are sitting. Do you tend to put one arm on the door or armrest? Drive with one hand? When sitting at a desk, do you lean to one side? Feel one seat bone more than the other? Sit in a chair in front of a mirror, or find some photos of you riding and look at how you sit. Is the distance between your shoulders and hips the same on both sides?

It is not unusual to have one side shorter than the other. Everyone is a bit asymmetrical and many people have a slight scoliosis. People who muck stalls right-handed are often stronger and longer on the left side of the torso. Collapsing on one side shortens the area between the ribs and pelvis (your "belt" or waist area). This could be caused by a contraction between the ribs, and/or a tilting of the entire rib cage to one side.

This is sometimes referred to as "collapsing the hip." That phrase, taken literally, is physically impossible unless your pelvis is broken! Either way, when one side is shortened, your weight will be unevenly distributed on the horse's back. When you lengthen both sides you will sit more squarely over your seat bones, your weight will be distributed more evenly, and your horse will be more balanced.

EXERCISE

On the Ground

Rather than sitting in the saddle, start by sitting on a flat chair or bench because it is easier to feel what happens to your seat. If possible, do this exercise in front of a mirror. Look to see which side of your rib cage is more collapsed, and which seat bone appears to have more weight on it (fig. 8.1). This may be the seat bone on the same side as the collapsed rib cage or the opposite seat bone. If you have a scoliosis, one seat bone may feel much more pronounced.

Raise one arm and extend your hand toward the ceiling (figs. 8.2 A & B). Make sure the fingers are long and your thumb is pointing behind you. Gently

8.1　The rider is collapsed in the ribs on the left side. Her left shoulder is lower than her right. Her belt is level therefore she has not collapsed in the waist.

8.2 A & B　The rider is softly reaching with her left arm in the air and lengthening through her side (A). This will even out the weight on her two seat bones. It is important to have your fingers lengthen upward with your thumb toward your back (B). This rotates the shoulder in the socket, creating more length in the arm and through the ribs.

8.3　The rider is more even in length through her two sides, from the armpit to the top of the pelvis.

reach for the ceiling. Feel how the rib and waist area open. Make sure you can breathe easily while you are reaching. If you can't, you are stretching your arm up too hard. Do the exercise a bit more gently.

Return your arm to your side and feel the distance from your armpit to the top of your pelvis. Notice how much longer your side feels. What has happened to the weight on your seat bones? Is it easier to breathe? Look in the mirror and see the difference between your two sides (fig. 8.3).

Repeat the process with the other arm. Only do one arm at a time, as there is a tendency to arch the back when you do both arms simultaneously. You want length through your sides without altering the length of your front and back (see Fix 7, p. 27, to find the middle between arching and rounding, and Fix 18, p. 72, for lengthening through the spine). Compare this side to the side you did first. Look in the mirror. Which arm overhead makes you more symmetrical?

On the Horse

Do this exercise on horseback at the halt. Put first one arm over your head, then bring it down and bring the other arm up. Feel what happens to your rib cage and your seat in the saddle. Is it the same as when you did the exercise sitting on a flat surface?

When you are ready, you can put one arm over your head at the walk, trot, and canter. Bring your hand down occasionally to let the circulation return to your fingers. Experiment with each arm in the different gaits. You might discover that the arm you like having over your head is more dominant but not the arm that is most effective when riding. Notice what happens to your horse when you lengthen through the rib and waist area on each side.

Strengthen Your Sides

9

Use this 5-Minute Fix to lengthen and strengthen both sides of your torso evenly. Do this exercise just before you ride to improve your straightness in the saddle. Remember the feeling of pulling on the band whenever you notice the urge to collapse.

Training Aids
Stretchy band, post

Do you:

- **Feel crooked when you ride?**

- **Cock one hip out to the side?**

- **Feel as if one side of your body is stronger?**

- **Feel like one hand wants to curl inward?**

- **Think one leg seems longer than the other?**

All of these problems may stem from your rib cage-to-hip connection. Here's a quick tip to help lengthen your sides, evenly tone your torso, control the wayward hip, and level your shoulders.

Notice what happens between your rib cage and pelvis (the waist area). Is one side shorter than the other? Do you collapse toward your right or left side? Does this correspond to the shoulder that is lower? Does the hand on the shortened side tend to curl inward? Do you use your arm and leg more

9.1   I am collapsed on my right side, causing my shoulders to appear unlevel. Trying to level my shoulders without correcting my torso is futile because that is addressing the symptom and not the cause.

strongly on the collapsed side in order to become more stable? Do you have trouble getting your horse to go straight or bend to the right or left?

When you collapse to one side, you shorten the distance between that shoulder, ribs, waist, and pelvis (fig. 9.1). Reach down sideways with one hand and feel that everything on this side moves closer together. This is important to do when you want to bend over to pick something up or tie your shoelaces, but not when trying to sit squarely in the saddle.

You want to strive for symmetry on your two sides so that you don't get thrown to one side as the horse moves. (If you have a scoliosis, take heart because by doing this exercise you can be *functionally straight* even when you are not physically straight.) Therefore, you need to be able to expand the ribs and create a firm connection between your torso, pelvis, and leg by lengthening through both sides.

EXERCISE

On the Ground

Test yourself to find out which side is easier to lengthen. Stand on one leg and then go up on your toes—still on that foot. Can you go up easily, without holding onto something? How long can you stay there without straining? Feel how you remain firm from your foot to your armpit in order to maintain your weight over the standing leg. You probably instinctively picked the leg you habitually stand on for this test.

Stand on the other foot and find out what happens. If this is the side you usually "collapse," it might not be so easy. Do you wobble, tilt, or lean on this leg? Typically, it is harder to stand over the collapsed side. Notice if your pelvis sways out to the side when standing on this leg.

This exercise will improve your ability to lengthen and become more stable on both sides. You will need some type of stretchy material. I use the black Equiband (see p. 198), but other materials will do (see Fix 32, p. 126). The stretchy band needs to be fairly strong but not overpowering. Alignment is more important than pulling on the band. If the band is too weak, you will

9.2　Use a stretchy band tied to something solid, like the fencepost here, for toning your sides.

9.3　Stand on one leg to increase the difficulty of the exercise. Start with the leg closest to the fence. Make sure you keep your pelvis square underneath you.

9.4　Incorrect: Don't let your body tilt or your pelvis sway out to the side!

9.5　To further increase the difficulty, stand on the leg furthest from the post. Keep the other leg away from the standing leg with the knee bent, and your foot behind and off the ground.

not feel any resistance. If it is too strong, you will throw your entire body into the exercise, which defeats the purpose. As you get stronger, you can increase the strength of the band by doubling it over, or you can get a stronger band.

Tie one end of the band to a solid object such as a fence. Stand about one foot away from the fence (fig. 9.2). Make sure the ground is level so you don't lean. Keep your shoulders down, elbows close to your sides and at a right angle (90 degrees) so your forearms are parallel to the ground while holding the band. With both feet on the ground, pull the band across your body, using your arms. Think of lengthening your spine as you pull. Slowly release the tension on the band and repeat several times (see Fix 1, p. 2, for ways to lengthen through the neck and head).

Turn to face the opposite direction and pull the band across your body again. Is it different when you face this direction?

Next, stand only on the foot closest to the post (fig. 9.3). Pull the band across your body. (You may need to decrease the band strength when you stand on one foot.) Slowly release the tension. Feel how much more stability you need through your side from pelvis to armpit when on one foot. Make sure you don't lean, tilt, or throw your hip out to the side (fig. 9.4). If you can work in front of a mirror, you can see if you are maintaining your alignment. Repeat, facing the other direction.

At first, you might find you cannot do this exercise at all. If this is the case, put the palm of your hand on the post and push against it as you pull the band. Think of lengthening upward as you pull. With practice, you will learn how to balance firmly on one leg without using the other hand for support.

To make the exercise more difficult, stand only on the leg furthest from the fence (fig. 9.5). Again decrease the band strength in the beginning and make sure you maintain your alignment.

On the Horse

In the saddle, remember the feeling of length and stability through both of your sides so that your weight is distributed evenly on both seat bones (fig. 9.6). Then return to your old position and find out how much the position of your ribs and pelvis has changed (see also Fix 15, p. 63, for help leveling your seat). Go back and forth a few times until the feeling of length becomes more comfortable. Ride in both new and old positions and find out how your horse responds. Which does he like better?

When you are stronger and more even through the sides of your body, your horse will track straighter and circles will become more symmetrical in both directions. (Combine this lesson with Fix 7 on p. 27 to create a frame for your torso with your front, back, and both sides forming a firm—but not rigid—rectangular box. Then add the lessons on the shoulder joints—Fix 22, p.88— and hip joints—Fix 19, p. 76—so there are four "wheels" at each corner of the box.)

9.6   My shoulders are level because I am even in length on both sides of my torso.

Pelvis and Lower Back

Introduction

The position of the *lower back* and *pelvis* is crucial for overall rider stability and mobility in the hips. This is the basis of a good seat—no matter what discipline you ride. When a rider's back is stiff or hollowed, or her hip joints are restricted, it directly affects the horse's ability to perform.

The same is true for the horse. The strength of the lower back, engagement of the pelvis, and freedom in the hip joints are what gives the horse the ability to lift the combined weight of rider and horse in dressage movements or over a jump.

I find that most riders were taught to ride with a hollowed back, which has destined them to grip with their legs, become tense, and pull on the reins to find stability. As you proceed with these exercises, go slowly. In the beginning, you will need to develop a sense of security in your new position. Once this happens you may find yourself reverting to your old position in times of stress until you have sufficient experience riding in a different way. If you have back pain, just do small amounts over days, or even weeks, rather than attempt to change your lower back position all at once. Remember to listen to your body as you make these changes. Review the Guidelines for Learning (p. xiv) as a reminder.

10 Finding Your Lower Back Position

Caution
If you have back pain, go slowly. Only do a small amount, for a short period of time, and see how you respond to the changes.

Stop
If this exercise increases your back pain at any time, do not continue.

Use this 5-Minute Fix to find a solid, flattened lower-back position. Regardless of discipline, you are more secure riding with a *flat* back.

Do you:

- Have trouble with your horse pulling you out of the saddle?

- Fall forward or back when jumping over a fence?

- Have a horse that travels with his head in the air?

Here's a quick tip to help you improve your stability in the saddle.

Take your reins in one hand. Place your other hand on your lower back (use the back of your hand as this will be easier on your shoulder). Feel your back. Is it hollowed, rounded, or flat? If you are unsure, look at photos or a video of yourself. A *hollowed* back pitches your weight forward, while a *rounded* position can cause you to fall back. Both may lead you to brace against the stirrups. A *flattened* back gives you the strength and stability you need for good riding (see photos on p. 45, and fig. 12.1, p. 52). This is especially important when jumping (see also Fix 18, p. 72, and Fix 24, p. 94, where you learn how to use your new back position to stop pulling back on the reins).

Comparable Parts:
The Lower Back

Human

The largest and most stable vertebrae in the human spine are the five lumbar vertebrae (between the thoracic spine and sacrum), located in the region referred to as the lower back. Most people have a forward curve, called *lordosis*, in this part of the spine, which is normal and necessary for standing and walking. Usually, this curve slightly decreases when we sit (figs. 10.1 A–C).

Horse

The lumbar portion of the horse's spine is the area behind your saddle between the last rib and the croup (fig. 10.1 D). Most horses have six lumbar vertebrae, though some Arabians have only five. The horse's lumbar spine has the ability to flex (round) and extend (hollow) like humans using similar flexor and extensor muscles. However, the horse is capable of rounding the back much more than we are, which is obvious when watching a horse doing a sliding stop or taking off over a large jump.

The horse needs to be able to round his lower back in order to lengthen his topline, lower his head, and engage his hindquarters. Pressure on the lumbar area causes the horse to hollow his lower back, which is one reason why his head will come up. Lumbar pressure can be caused by many things, most commonly: a badly fitting or poorly placed saddle; a rider sitting in a hollow-backed position; or a rider sitting too far back in the saddle. It is important to correct the way your saddle fits and your riding position in order for your horse to use his lower back effectively.

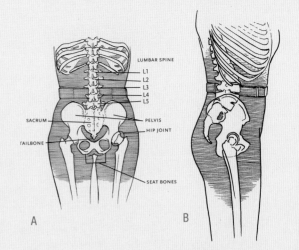

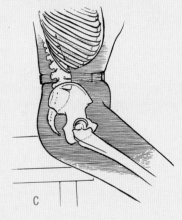

10.1 A–D   The human lower back and pelvis viewed from the rear (A). The lower back—the lumbar spine area—generally has more forward curve when you are standing than when sitting (B). It is normal for this forward curve to flatten slightly when you sit (C). Compare this to the lumbar spine and pelvis of an Arabian (D).

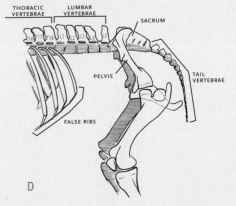

EXERCISE

On the Ground

You can alter the amount of lumbar curve by *hollowing* (extending) or *rounding* (flexing) your back.

When you *hollow* your back, the *extensor* muscles (sometimes called "anti-gravity muscles") contract, increasing its forward curve. While sitting on a flat surface with your feet squarely on the floor, feel these extensors by placing your fingers on each side of your spine. Change the shape of your lower back noticing that as you hollow, the muscles narrow, and as you decrease the curve, they broaden. In some people, these back muscles are so taut they feel like cables running along each side of the spine.

When you *round* your back, the *flexor* muscles contract causing the lumbar curve to decrease, while at the same time the extensor muscles gradually relax. You cannot feel the flexors (primarily *psoas major* and *minor*) because they lie along the inside of the spine behind your internal organs. (You can find them in the grocery store though, commonly known as filet mignon and tenderloin!)

When your lower back is *flat*, the forward curve of the lumbar spine is stabilized by both flexor and extensor muscles.

On the Horse

To find your solid, flat lower-back position on your horse, first check that you are sitting in the middle of your saddle. Then, gently hollow and round your back (figs. 10.2 A & B). Make very small, slow, movements so that you can sense and feel what is happening. Notice that your seat bones change position in the saddle as you move your lower back. Feel how your back muscles change shape, texture, and tone as you move. Be careful. A little movement can feel good but you can make yourself sore when you do too much.

Find the place where your seat bones are pointing down and your back is flat (fig. 10.3). Consciously change your seat bone position and feel how this affects your lower back. Notice the amount of tension you have in your abdominal area with each small change. See if you can alter the position of

10.2 A & B   In A, the rider's back is hollowed. She is sitting forward on her crotch and will be unable to stop the horse from pulling her out of the saddle. In B, the rider's back is rounded and her weight is on the back of the saddle. This can make the horse quite uncomfortable.

10.3   The rider with a flat back. She is solid in the saddle and will not need to use the reins for security. (Note, her arms are in this position for the purposes of the photograph only.)

your pelvis *without* intentionally contracting your abdominal muscles (see sidebar, p. 46). Notice how this affects the freedom of your hips. Sense if they feel more open or if your legs feel longer.

If your back was very hollowed to start with, you may notice a significant difference in your horse when you change position. Your flat back will make it possible for the horse to put his head down. You will ease the pressure on his back; take weight off his forehand; and allow him to use his lumbar area more effectively. Finding your flat back position also gives you more freedom in the hips, thus allowing your horse to move more easily under you (see also Fix 19, p. 76).

Functional Intelligence versus Conscious Control

Many riders mistakenly think that tense abdominal muscles (often achieved by pulling the belly button toward the spine) are necessary in order to ride well. If this were true, little children would not be able to ride! They have a belly that sticks out yet they can sit, stand, run, and ride in a very natural and correct position. Why is this? They are using the muscles designed to maintain an upright posture. In children, this postural system functions *without conscious thought*. Most adults compromise this coordinated action by spending many hours driving the car or sitting in front of a computer.

An exercise program is important to reestablish good overall muscle tone and coordination. Overdevelopment and overuse of the abdominal muscles by constantly contracting the belly button toward the spine can restrict pelvic and hip movement, and lead to back, leg, and hip pain. The abdominal muscles, while part of the postural muscle system, need to work *in conjunction* with other muscles.

Muscles *only* contract when they receive a signal from the nervous system. Cut the nerve to a muscle and it will wither away because it no longer receives an impulse. If you had to consciously think about all the muscles required for a "simple" action, like getting out of a chair, you would never stand up. The complexity of this basic function is more than you can consciously control. Intentionally thinking about when and what muscles are working is inefficient and distracting to the function—proper action—of riding.

By focusing on overall alignment and function you let your intelligent brain send the required signals to the muscles for each and every movement. As you refine your function you will increase efficiency, minimize muscular effort, and *you will not have to think about* what muscles are working. Just like a child, your body will be able to do what is necessary for the task at hand *without conscious thought*.

A Solid Solution for a "Soggy" Back

11

Use this 5-Minute Fix to improve your back position both on the horse and in the car (and maybe even for the rest of your life). As you become more "confirmed" in a good back alignment, you will find it is easier to sit more comfortably and carry your head with less effort.

Do you:

- **Have a very flexible back?**

- **Switch from a slumping position to sitting up too straight with your back hollowed?**

- **Sometimes wish you had a little support so you'd know where your back is supposed to be?**

Here's a quick tip to help you find a good back position.

Next time you ride, notice what happens to your back. Does it feel unstable? Are you having a hard time figuring out if you are in a good alignment? Do you *think* you are straight only to find out later from photos, videos, or your instructor that you aren't? Or, are you still simply unaware of what you are looking for (figs. 11.1 A & B)?

Training Aids
A gardener's "kneeling" pad; Ace® bandage

Caution
Even though the ace bandage stretches and does not prevent you from moving your arms, test it off the horse to be sure. The idea of having your arms bound to your sides may cause you some anxiety. If so, tie the kneeling pad around your torso with your arms *outside* the bandage, or skip this lesson altogether.

11.1 A & B This rider is very flexible—she can easily round (A) or hollow (B) her back.

What's Holding Up Your Head?

The position of your back is critical for good riding. At one end of your spine is your head, a 10- to 15-pound "bowling ball," while at the other end is the pelvis, the counterweight to the head (see Fixes 1 and 10, pp. 2 and 42). In between is the spine, which is somewhat flexible. The large muscles of the lower back and pelvic region are designed for doing the majority of the weight-bearing work. The neck muscles are small, designed for orienting the head—looking up, down, and around. If the weight of your head is not well supported by your spine, you are going to stiffen other parts of the body in an attempt to absorb the shocks created by the horse's movement.

When your back is well aligned, you will feel more solid and secure in the saddle. This stability transmits to the horse, giving him a sense of security, too. It allows him to find his balance underneath you.

You have a clear mental image of your front view because you are so used to looking at your posture in a mirror. You think you are sitting up straight because you can see that your chest is up. It is difficult to tell if your back is in good alignment because you don't have an image of it. You may think that you

11.2 A–C With the kneeling pad in place, I have wrapped an ace bandage around the rider's midsection (A). In this case, I have wound the bandage around her elbows to add support to her back with her upper arms. The kneeling pad gives the rider feedback so she can tell when her back is in good alignment—seen here from side and rear view (B & C).

are well aligned, but your back is actually hollowed. What you need is some objective feedback to help you *feel* when your back is in a better position. For this, you need a couple of items.

Rummage around and find an ace bandage and a fairly firm kneeling pad—the type that gardeners use. You can find one at any garden center, if not in your own potting shed. You might need an assistant to help you get started with this lesson.

EXERCISE

On the Horse

If you have a quiet horse and someone to help you, mount first. Use the ace bandage for attaching the pad to your back (figs. 11.2 A–C). Test the stretch in the ace bandage so you know you can still move your arms (see also fig. 23.5, p. 93). It is important that you don't feel "trapped." (Note: If you are by yourself, put the pad around your waist in the front of your body before you mount and then slide it around to your back.) You can choose to have your arms outside or inside the ace bandage. I realize this isn't much of a fashion statement but it does work!

Because the pad is basically a flat item, you can feel when your back is flattened as opposed to being rounded or hollowed. Notice the places where the pad touches your back…and where it doesn't. Of course, some of this is due to the natural curves of your spine. But you might find, if you take a moment to explore the contact the pad is offering, that you can actually spread the contact over more of the pad by making slight changes to your lower back position.

For the next few rides, wear the pad while going through your normal routine, and let the pad give you a gentle reminder of where you are and where you want your back to be. After a few times, ride without the pad but remember the feeling of what it was like to have it there.

Utilize That "Sitting Time" to Your Riding Advantage

In general, it is important to develop good sitting posture. If you are like the majority of riders you spend more time off your horse than on. Don't waste all that good "sitting time" when off your horse; put it to good use. When sitting on something that doesn't give you any back support, use the back pad from this lesson to remind you of the posture you would like to maintain on your horse.

You probably spend a lot of time in the car. You need support there, too, since most car seats are not designed to encourage good riding posture. Help your riding by adjusting the base of the car seat so it is as level as possible and set the seat back so it is upright. Keep a towel or a small diameter foam roll (like the one used in Fix 47, p. 184) in the car. Roll the towel up like a tube and place it lengthwise down your spine—starting below the base of your neck—between the car seat and your back. Like the kneeling pad, it gives you support when you are driving and helps you develop good habits for riding.

Back Up Your Heel Position **12**

Use this 5-Minute Fix to feel the connection from your back to your heels. Next time you are fighting to get your heels down remind yourself to flatten your back and allow the weight to sink into your heels.

> **Do you:**
>
> - Have trouble keeping your heels down?
>
> - Find they creep up even after you have jammed them down?
>
> - Constantly hear your instructor yelling "Heels Down!"?
>
> - Have one heel that comes up more than the other?
>
> - Wish you could do something about it?

Here's a quick tip to help you keep your heels deep.

Next time you ride notice what happens to your heels. Are they above, at, or below the level of your stirrup? How much weight is on your toes? Are you bracing against the stirrup to get your heels down? What happens when you shorten your stirrups? Do you stiffen all over trying to keep your heels where they belong? Do you feel unsteady no matter how hard you jam your heels down?

12.1 An excellent example of a "light seat" over ground poles. Notice the rider's solid, flat back, and her crisp angles at the elbow, hip, knee, and ankle. There is a straight line from elbow to bit and the angle of the forearm matches the angle of the thigh. The rider's weight is sinking into her heel without her jamming the lower leg forward. The ankle is well placed under her hip with her buttocks back in the saddle counterbalancing the angle of the upper body, which is correctly inclined forward from the hip. Her eyes are looking forward because her base of support is solid. (Note: The towels under the flaps of the saddle provide thigh contact in order to achieve this solid position—see Fix 31, p. 122.)

Heels Down

It is unfortunate that most riders are taught to get their heels down incorrectly. Instead of learning to sink their weight into their heels, they typically end up bracing against the stirrups, straightening their knees, then leaning forward in an attempt to balance over their feet. In this position, their ankles remain rigid. People spend hours trying to stretch their calves; buy hinged stirrups (which can make matters worse); or resign themselves to being unable to achieve this most basic tenet of a good riding position. When they brace the lower leg forward or jam their foot against the stirrup, a tremendous amount of tension is created that must be resolved first in order to have a solid, deep heel.

A secure *heels down,* providing the rider with a good base of support, comes from a solid, flat back position and supple, relaxed joints—particularly the hips, knees, and ankles (fig. 12.1, and see also figs. 18.3 and 32.6, pp. 75 and 131). When your back is hollowed, you won't be able to get your weight into your heels correctly, no matter how hard you try. Your leg weight must "fall" through the heel in a direction toward the horse's hind foot—with your knee bent—in order to achieve *heels down*. How deep your heel actually goes is more a function of stirrup length and much less important than *the way* in which your weight goes into your heel.

When you have a "deep" heel your foot rests on the stirrup and your calf touches your horse's sides—that is, when his conformation allows (see Fix 29, p. 114). You will then be able to apply calf pressure to give your horse a leg aid. When you need a stronger aid, you can make your calf muscles firmer by flexing your ankle—as long as you keep your knee bent and don't let your lower leg swing forward.

The purpose of flexing the ankle is to tone the calf muscle creating a stronger leg aid when used against the horse's sides, which is separate from heels down (see sidebar, p. 52). When your ankle is already flexed to the maximum so that your heel is as far as it will go, you lose the ability to refine your leg aids into softer or stronger signals. Instead, you will always be "shouting" at your horse with your legs, which can make him dull and unresponsive. When this happens, most riders have to resort to using artificial aids like a whip or spurs in order to get the horse to move.

EXERCISE

On the Ground

The alignment of your lower back determines whether your weight falls into your heel or toward the front of your foot. Here's an exercise derived from *Bones for Life*®, a program developed by Ruthy Alon based on the Feldenkrais Method® to teach people how to organize their skeleton into a safe weight-bearing posture in order to maintain bone health. This exercise will help you understand the connection between your lower back and heels.

Stand with your feet in a "step position" (one foot ahead of the other about hip-width apart). Make sure your knees are bent. Place the back of one hand on your lower back. Hollow your back and feel how your weight moves toward the front of both feet (fig. 12.2). Now flatten your back and feel how the weight shifts into your heels (fig. 12.3). Change your foot position and see what happens when you have the other foot forward.

Shift your body over your front foot and feel how this tends to hollow your back, transferring your weight to the front of your feet again. (This is a normal event when walking.) Bring your body back and while still in the step position, lift the front of the forward foot and jam your heel into the ground. Feel how your lower back hollows, your knee straightens, and you lean forward with your upper body (fig. 12.4). This is just what happens when you jam your heels down against the stirrup, except that in the saddle, you wind up swinging your lower leg forward and pushing your buttocks back toward the cantle.

12.2 Hollowing my back shifts my weight forward onto the front leg and toward the toes of both feet.

12.3 In "step position," my back is flat and the weight is sinking into the heel of my back foot (left heel).

12.4 Lifting the front of my forward foot and pressing into the heel is essentially the same as bracing against the stirrup. My knee straightens, which pushes my pelvis back and up, and causes my back to hollow.

12.5 I sink deeper by bending my knees—in effect, shortening the stirrups if I were in the saddle. My back lengthens and even more weight goes into my back heel.

Now, flatten your back in the step position again. As you flatten, let your knees and hips bend. Feel how your back lengthens. The weight transfers across the whole foot and into the heel of the back foot. Notice how your pelvis comes underneath you (fig. 12.5). This allows your seat to come forward into the deepest part of the saddle. Your weight will sink down through both heels making your base of support very stable (see also Fix 32, p. 126, for additional help when in the saddle).

An Easy Way to Flatten Your Hollow Back

Use this 5-Minute Fix to rest for a few minutes and let gravity help you find a flat, solid back position. You can use this exercise to reduce the tension in your lower back, especially when it is feeling a bit sore—or take this time to visualize yourself riding.

Training Aids
Small towel, string or Equistrap, book for under head

> **Do you:**
>
> • **Tend to have a hollowed back when you ride?**
>
> • **Think that you can't change it?**
>
> • **Have back pain?**
>
> • **Have a hard time on long rides?**

Maybe you have been taught to hollow your back but didn't realize that this position can put your horse on his forehand. Perhaps you just don't know how to change this habit. Here's a way to relax your back so that you can have a solid position in the saddle, in just a few minutes each day.

Next time you ride, place the back of one hand on the waist area of your lower back. Notice if this area is hollowed, rounded, or flattened. Feel if there is any tension in your hips. Do you grip the horse's sides with your legs? Is your horse on his forehand? Intentionally hollow your back a bit and feel what happens to you and your horse.

The Lumbar Curve

The five lumbar vertebrae of the lower back have a forward curve—called *lumbar lordosis*. The bottommost vertebra joins the sacrum at the lumbosacral joint, connecting the spine to the pelvis (see figs. 10.1 A & B, p. 43). A baby is born without a lumbar lordosis: it begins to form as he learns to lift his head and look up. As the baby continues to develop, eventually learning to stand, the lumbar curve becomes observable at around three to four years of age, and is fully formed around the age of 10 (fig. 13.1).

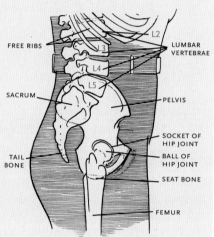

13.1 The lumbar spine and sacrum viewed from the side. Notice the depth of the sacrum from front to back.

Along with the other naturally occurring curves in the spine, this lumbar curve is essential for standing. The curves provide the strength and stability for the spine to carry the weight of the upper body and head. However, too much of a good thing creates discomfort.

Due to poor posture; sitting in chairs; social environments (think about how teenagers stand); and activities like gymnastics; this lumbar curve can become exaggerated. Once established, the image of a very curved lower back becomes fixed, resulting in a belief by some that this excessive curve can't change. This is far from the truth.

I am a testament to how much the back can change and how much healthier it is *not to* accentuate the lumbar curve. In 1979, I suffered a crippling back injury. I was in bed for months. Over time I recovered, and since then I have learned how to develop a healthy back with the strength needed for riding without pain. I used the technique described in this 5-Minute Fix for many years as part of my rehabilitation to achieve this result.

Sitting versus Standing

Please be aware that your posture when sitting in the saddle should not be the same as that when standing on the ground. When you sit, the lumbar curve decreases slightly—unless the muscles are so tight that your back can't let go (see fig. 10.1 C, p. 43). When riding you need the flexibility of the lower back to help absorb the horse's motion. And, an overly tight back will restrict your horse from moving freely.

EXERCISE

On the Ground

A hollow back posture transfers to your horse and puts him on the forehand. A flatter back helps you both be more comfortable, work less, and yet do more. To feel how your lumbar spine can change shape, stand up. Put your hand on your lower back and feel the forward curve that goes from the pelvis to the rib area. Sense how much curve there is when standing. Increase the forward curve slightly by tilting the top of your pelvis forward and down (*anterior tilt*).

Now sit on a soft cushioned chair or couch and find out if your lower back "rounds" (*posterior tilt*) taking on the shape of the back of the chair or the cushions. Most people don't realize how much their lower back rounds when they sit on a sofa or in a car seat.

If your sitting posture is overly hollowed, give your back muscles a chance to relax. Use the following Alexander Technique exercise, called "The Alexander Lie Down," for a few minutes every day.

Lie on the floor with your knees bent and feet flat on the ground. Note the gap between your lower back and the floor (fig. 13.2). When the gap is significant and your lower back is uncomfortable, place a small towel under your belt area (fig. 13.3). If your knees want to fall away from each other, take a necktie or piece of string and tie your thighs together just above your knees (fig. 13.4). This way you will not have to use any muscular effort to keep your knees upright. If your knees want to fall in together, put a small pillow between them.

13.2 A tense, hollow lower back. Notice the belt area comes away from the bodywork table.

13.3 For comfort, place a small towel under your lower back so that you fill in the space between your back and the floor.

13.4 Tie your knees together if they want to fall away from each other. Leave the string loose enough so your knees are still about hip-width apart. This will alleviate the muscular effort involved in holding your knees upright so that you can relax more fully.

13.5 The lower back has now relaxed and flattened against the table.

Now lie here for about 15 minutes (even 5 minutes is better than none). "Breathe into" the area of your lower back. Imagine the "free" ribs (the ones not attached to the sternum) expanding as you breathe (see Fix 6, p. 22). Allow gravity to do the work for you while you rest on the floor. You can listen to music to help you relax.

Feel the quality of your back muscles while you are lying down. You want them to feel spongy, like a hard-boiled egg without the shell. You may find that, as your back muscles let go, you will need to remove the towel (fig. 13.5). In this position you are practicing good riding posture and using gravity to your advantage!

When ready, slowly roll to your side and stand up. Notice how you feel when standing. Particularly note the relaxation in your lower back area. A few minutes a day may alleviate any back pain you have and will make a big difference to your riding.

14 Collecting Yourself

••••

Use this 5-Minute Fix to help you feel what it is like to sit deep in the saddle. When you allow your back to lengthen and your sacrum to "hang down," you will find that it is easier to sit at all gaits.

Training Aids
Waist pouch, weights

Caution
Be careful when wearing the weights. Make sure the belt is snug enough that the weights do not bounce.

Stop
Do not do this lesson if you have back problems, such as pinched nerves, slipped discs, or other conditions. Remove the weight belt immediately if you feel any pain.

Do you:

- **Have trouble keeping your balance in the saddle?**

- **Tend to pitch forward?**

- **Have difficulty sitting to the canter?**

- **Wish your seat felt deeper without making you feel tense?**

Here is a simple solution to give you a sense of lengthening through your back and sinking deep in the saddle.

Next time you ride notice what happens to your seat in all gaits. Do you feel as if you can't sit *down* in the saddle? Does your horse fall on the forehand? Do you brace against your stirrups to feel secure? When you put one hand on your lower back, is it hollowed?

In order to sit deep in the saddle, your sacrum—the flat triangular bone that forms the rear portion of your pelvis—needs to hang down (figs. 14.1 A–C). The sacrum can't hang down when you hollow your back or stick your seat bones out behind you (fig. 14.2). (To learn more about your lower back, see Fix 29, p. 114.)

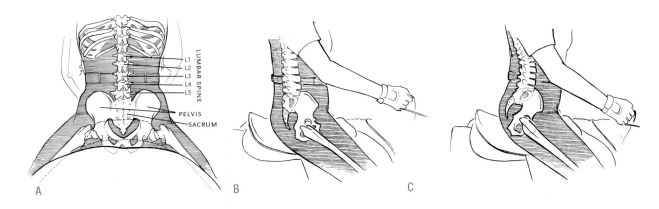

14.1 A–C   The pelvis and sacrum, as seen from the rear on the saddle (A). Viewed from the side, the pelvis is level and the sacrum is hanging down (B). Here, the pelvis has tipped forward and down (C). The sacrum is tipped up and out behind.

Knowing you have to flatten your back to let your sacrum hang down is one thing. Doing this while riding isn't always that easy to accomplish. To help get this feeling, find a pouch that you can strap around your waist and add some weights to it. I use an old ski-patrol belt and lead saddle-pad weights (fig. 14.3). You can use any kind of pack or pouch that attaches to your waist and shapes to your back. The weights can be ankle weights, even bags of rice, or anything else that is dense and heavy.

EXERCISE

On the Horse

Begin with a pound or two of weights; you can always add more later. Place the pouch low around your waist so that the weights rest on your sacrum. Make sure you secure it snugly so it doesn't bounce around when you ride (figs. 14.4 A & B).

Mount your horse and at the halt take a minute to observe how the weight gently asks you to lengthen your back and sink into the saddle. If this feels

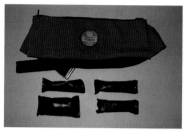

14.2   This rider's sacrum is tipped up, her seat bones are out behind her, and her back is hollow.

14.3   Use some kind of pouch or pack (in this case, an old ski-patrol pack) and some heavy, but not lumpy, weights. These are the lead weights from a racing saddle pad.

14.4 A & B   Place the pouch or pack low on your waist so that the weights rest on your sacrum. Make sure the belt is snug.

14.5   After using the weighted pouch, the rider's seat bones are under her and her back is lengthened.

painful or uncomfortable, reduce the amount of weight or remove the belt altogether.

Ride at the walk making sure that the pouch doesn't shift around. The weight should merely *suggest* that you drop your sacrum into the saddle to deepen your seat. Ride at the trot—and eventually the canter—when you are ready. Notice how these well-placed weights help you sit the canter and give you a feeling of security and stability—essentially, they lower your center of gravity (fig. 14.5).

Remember, for the horse to collect himself he must lower his hindquarters (pelvis). In order for you to collect your horse, *you must collect yourself*—allow your sacrum to hang down (not overly tuck) to deepen your seat in the saddle. As you become familiar with the feeling remove the weights and see if you can find the same feeling of depth that you had with them.

How to Level Your Seat

Use this 5-Minute Fix whenever you feel you are sitting more heavily on one seat bone. When your seat is level, your horse will be more responsive, turn better in both directions, and be more willing to lift his back up underneath you.

Training Aid
Washcloth or small towel

Caution
Be aware when riding with the washcloth under your seat. If it works its way loose, it could startle your horse.

Do you:

- **Feel one seat bone more than the other?**

- **Slide off one side of your saddle?**

- **Have one leg that always sticks further forward than the other?**

- **Find your horse drifts or bulges to one direction?**

Here's a quick tip to help you level your seat.

Next time you ride, get a sense of your two seat bones. Do you feel one more strongly or only feel one instead of two? Does it feel as if your seat is lower on one side? Is this pattern consistent regardless of the direction you are riding? Or, does it feel worse when going to the right—or left—but less noticeable the other way? The cause could be one of three possibilities, or a combination of all three: your horse's back isn't level; the seat of your saddle isn't level; or you are not sitting level in your saddle.

15.1 This rider's seat is not level, dropping off on the right side. Notice that the seam of her britches does not line up with the center of the saddle, which is level and in line with the horse's spine.

When your horse rotates his rib cage or his back isn't muscled evenly, the saddle will be lower on one side. Your seat will mirror the saddle's position unless you intentionally compensate for this problem. A horse is able to rotate his rib cage just like a human. When you rotate your rib cage, you turn to look behind you (rotating on a *vertical axis*). When the horse rotates his rib cage, his sternum is no longer pointing toward the ground, and one side of his back moves down while the other side comes up (rotating on a *horizontal axis*). This is often referred to as "dropping a shoulder" and can make the saddle unlevel. When the horse's rib cage and spine are not rotated, the withers are upright.

Many riders don't realize that sitting unlevel can be caused by the horse's body so they keep trying to adjust themselves. For example, you may feel as if one stirrup is always longer than the other, but when you measure your leathers they are the same length. Or, you may notice you don't have this problem when riding other horses in the same saddle (see Fix 28, p. 110, for information on measuring leathers). Both are good clues that the horse may be the problem. If the horse's rib cage is not rotated and the muscling is even on the two sides of his back, you need to look for another cause for your unlevel seat.

A good indication that your unlevel feeling is the saddle's "fault" is if the problem goes away when you ride in a *different saddle* on the same horse. If your seat is the cause, the sensations and feelings you observe will be relatively similar in different saddles and on different horses (fig. 15.1). Take a look at the seat of your saddle. Have you worn a dent or groove into one side?

EXERCISE

On the Horse

Whatever the cause, you can help reduce—or perhaps solve—this problem with an ordinary washcloth or small piece of toweling. Fold it in half and place it under the seat bone you think is lower (figs. 15.2 A & B). Ride at the walk (you will lose the cloth at the rising trot) and notice if this feels better or worse. Then, double the cloth and test it again. Keep folding the cloth so it is thicker until it feels as if you have too much underneath your seat.

Now, remove the towel altogether to remind yourself what your seat felt like earlier. Evaluate whether you feel better—or worse—with the toweling. How is your horse responding? Is he raising his back or getting more hollow? Did you fall into a "hole" when you took the cloth away?

Repeat the process, placing the cloth underneath the other seat bone. Does this feel better or worse? How does your horse respond? Does it feel better with the cloth under this seat bone or the other one? Do you and your horse agree?

Again, place the washcloth under the low seat bone. Find the thickness that feels just right and ride a bit longer at different gaits. Some of my students put the cloth inside their pants or breeches so they can post the trot and canter. Be creative in finding a way to keep the washcloth in place. You won't have to keep the cloth there forever; once you feel the difference, you will want to keep the sensation of a level seat—and the difference in your horse will be the best reminder!

When you ride without the towel, recall the feeling of what it was like under your seat. Remember how your horse felt when you sat more level. Notice how you change your position and support yourself on other parts of your seat and legs to recreate this feeling and how your horse is more willing to lift up his back and fill in underneath you.

At first you might use the toweling every day. After a while, a once-a-week reminder will keep you on track. (Use Fixes 1 and 5, pp. 2 and 17, in combination with this lesson to lengthen through your head and neck.)

15.2 A & B The rider has placed a folded washcloth underneath her right seat bone. When you look at the washcloth under the rider's seat from the side, you can see that she is using several layers (A). You will have to experiment to find out what works best for you. Observe that now she is sitting level on the saddle (B). Her britches' seam lines up with the middle of the cantle. There is marked improvement in her alignment all the way up through her shoulders.

16 Have a Ball Finding Your Horse's Forward Movement

Training Aid
Exercise ball

Caution
When you use the exercise ball on a slippery surface such as a tile floor or cement, be aware that it could slide out from underneath you. If you use your ball at the barn, keep the horses in mind—it might frighten them.

Use this 5-Minute Fix to ensure you are *allowing* your horse to move forward freely before you *ask* him to do so.

> **Do you:**
>
> • **Have difficulty getting your horse to go forward?**
>
> • **Try "pumping" with your seat; kicking; squeezing; spurs; whips; and any other means at your disposal, but the horse still won't go?**
>
> • **Find that other people have the same problem on your horse, or is it only you?**

While it is true that you may need artificial aids (spurs or a whip) on a lazy horse, the answer to the problem may not be *what* you are doing but *how* you are doing it. When you want the horse to go forward, you need to take the "handbrake" off your legs and seat.

First, I want to explain the idea of *going forward*. Simply "moving" is not necessarily "going forward." Susan Harris, in *The United States Pony Club Manual of Horsemanship Intermediate Horsemanship C Level*, gives a good clear description of free, forward moment: "In free forward movement he [the horse] is willing to move forward easily from a light leg aid, and he uses his body well when he moves. A pony that lacks free forward movement might act lazy, stubborn, or reluctant to move; or he may move with short, 'sticky' strides."

Ms. Harris continues to describe a horse in free, forward movement as "not fast but long even strides, using his hindquarters, back, and muscles freely with each stride. It also means that he wants to go forward and to do what you ask but is calm and relaxed about it."

EXERCISE

On the Ground

How is free forward movement accomplished? The first thing you need to check is whether your seat and legs are preventing your horse from moving. To do this, you need an appropriately sized exercise ball, which means you want a 90-degree angle at the back of your knee when sitting on the top of the ball. If the ball is too big, you will have to brace with your legs like you do on a "downhill" saddle or low-withered horse in order to stay on. If the ball is too small, you will feel as if you are sitting in a "hole" as you do when on an "uphill" saddle or a very hollow-backed horse.

Make sure your feet are a hip-width apart. Do not try to straddle the ball; this restricts your hips. Begin to roll the ball. What direction are you choosing first? Is it a side-to-side, or a forward-and-backward movement? If it is sideways, this may be a big reason why your horse won't go forward (fig. 16.1)! When your seat constantly moves to the left and right, the horse has to try and stay under you. This would be like your trying to balance a jar on the top of your head when it is wobbling all over.

In order for the horse to go forward, you need to direct your seat forward. Begin to roll the ball forward and back. Notice if your inclination is to roll the ball more forward (the angle at the back of the knee decreases) or more backward (the angle at the back of the knee increases). Have someone watch you to be sure. If you unconsciously roll the ball more backward than forward, you may be making it hard for your horse to move forward (see Fix 12, p.51, for more on bending your knees).

When you roll backward from the 90-degree angle, you are straightening

16.1 This rider's seat is rolling the exercise ball sideways, which if done when in the saddle will cause the horse to "waddle" instead of march forward.

16.2 The rider is pushing the ball backward, a motion that in the saddle will block the horse's forward movement. Notice that her knees are quite straight and her feet are bracing against the ground.

your knees and bracing slightly against the ground (fig. 16.2). When you do this in the saddle, you are pushing against your stirrups (see Fix 32, p. 126, for help with this in the saddle).This presses your seat toward the cantle, thus preventing your horse from going forward. It is like having your foot on the brake and trying to step on the accelerator at the same time.

Now make a conscious effort to let the ball roll further forward than back so that the angle of your knees decreases (fig. 16.3). Make sure you keep your feet flat on the ground. Return to the midpoint with your knees at 90 degrees and roll forward again, each time decreasing the angle at the back of your knees. Find a rhythm.

Before you ride, spend a few moments rolling the ball from 90 degrees, forward. This serves as a good reminder to allow your knees to move slightly forward and down as you ride. This is a very small but important movement because it tells your horse you want him to move forward. Then, your other aids will have a more positive effect.

Working movements out on the exercise ball can really improve your riding since the ball is "objective" and only does what you do. For more exercises on the ball, refer to my DVD, *Ride Like A Natural Part 3: Get on the Equiball* (see p. 198).

16.3 Here, the rider is allowing the ball to move forward by letting her knees bend so that the knee angle is less than 90 degrees, while keeping her feet flat on the ground. When in the saddle, her knees would move slightly forward and down with each stride.

Sitting the Canter

17

Use this 5-Minute Fix to sit to the canter. By using your free hand in various locations on the saddle, you will find the swing in your seat that let's you sit.

Caution
Be careful when riding with your hand pinned under your seat.

Stop
Remove your hand from under your seat if your horse needs attention or you feel unstable, especially on turns.

Do you:

- **Have trouble sitting your horse's canter?**

- **Hear and feel your buttocks slapping the saddle?**

- **Brace against the stirrups in order to sit down?**

Here's a quick tip to get you going with the flow and staying in the saddle at the canter.

Notice what happens when you canter. Do you stiffen and brace to get your heels down? Do you push your feet forward? Do you have air space between you and the saddle? Does your horse object to cantering by tossing his head in the air and hollowing his back? He may be doing this because you are slapping the saddle with each stride or not following the canter motion.

Problems May Be Signs of Pain

The horse needs to be able to lift his withers and "round" his back in order to canter comfortably under saddle. If for some reason he can't do this because the saddle hurts; he has some existing pain in his back; or from improper shoeing, you will find it difficult to sit the canter. It is vital to address these issues. If your horse is tense, jarring, rushing, or extremely hollow at the canter, have a veterinarian, farrier, saddle-fitter, or therapist determine what is causing the pain.

17.1　I have placed the back of my hand on my lower back to make sure it feels "full."

17.2　Second, I place my hand on the cantle, pushing against the saddle to keep my pelvis from slipping back and instead encourage it to move forward with the swing of the horse's back.

In canter, the horse's back has a forward-and-up motion similar to the *forward* portion of a swing's trajectory. When you follow the forward swing, your pelvis should go with the movement of the horse's back: an under-forward-up motion. Tight hips, bracing against the stirrups, a hollow back, and/or pitching forward all prevent you from following the forward motion. Instead, you are simulating the *backward* part of the swing's trajectory, which prevents the horse from lifting his back (see also Fix 16, p. 65, for more on this). Use the following exercise to get in sync with your horse at the canter.

EXERCISE

On the Horse

You will place your hand in four locations during this exercise. I suggest you review these placements at the walk first, before cantering.

Put both reins in your outside (closest to the arena fence or wall) hand. Place your inside hand (palm facing out) on your lower back (fig. 17.1). "Fill into" your hand so that your back is full and flat (review Fix 10, p. 42). While keeping your back flat, move your hand to the cantle of the saddle palm side down (fig. 17.2). Press against the cantle. You might feel as if you have to lean back a bit to reach, which is okay as long as your horse continues to canter.

The third position is placing this hand underneath your buttocks, palm side up (fig. 17.3). Press your hand firmly to your buttocks so that they move together. Use your hand to encourage the under-forward-up swing motion of the canter, toward the horse's ears. You do not want your buttocks sliding over your hand, you want your hand and buttocks to move together.

The fourth placement is to put your hand, palm side down, on the seat of the saddle so that your pelvis rides over your hand, still following the under-forward-up swing motion (fig. 17.4).

Continue cantering and return your hand to your lower back. Repeat the hand-placement cycle of lower back, cantle, buttocks, seat of the saddle, moving your hand to the next position after several strides. Do not change locations too quickly. Take some time in each position to find and feel the swing motion.

Once you get the idea on one lead, stop and change direction. Repeat the cycle: lower back, cantle, buttocks, and seat of the saddle. Then reverse it so you go from the seat of the saddle to your buttocks, cantle, and lower back. You might find that one place doesn't help you as much but another placement makes a big difference. Keep your hand in that critical spot for a few more strides and see if you can "roll with the canter" a bit more clearly. Then, remove your hand and find out if you can follow the motion of the canter while holding both reins. Eventually, simply holding the reins in one hand may help you recall the under-forward-up feeling.

17.3   Third, I have my hand underneath my buttocks, palm up. The hand and the buttocks stay connected and follow the canter's swing.

17.4   Finally, I stick my hand to the seat of the saddle, palm down, so that my pelvis slides over my hand.

18

Improve Your Forward Position

Use this 5-Minute Fix as a body-position warm-up whenever you are going to need your forward position. If you only ride on the flat, this lesson will be useful to teach you how to lengthen through your spine.

> **Do you:**
>
> - Feel insecure or fall forward when in the jumping position?
>
> - Find your horse speeds up—or slows down—when approaching a jump?
>
> - Have trouble with your horse stopping at cross-rails or logs when you attempt to take your weight off his back?
>
> - Have trouble going uphill?

Here's a quick tip to improve your balance and your horse's performance when you are in a forward position.

Whether you ride young horses, jump, or trail ride, having a solid forward position is essential to allowing your horse to move freely under you. A good forward seat keeps your weight over the horse's center of gravity, while the joints in your legs (hips, knees, and ankles) absorb the horse's motion (see also Fix 50, p. 194).

If you pitch forward, fold at the waist, or round or hollow your back, you will put weight onto the horse's forehand, making it harder for him to balance himself over a log, a jump, or just traveling uphill.

Names for Different Seats and Riding Positions

When I was a kid growing up in Fairfield County, Connecticut (a hotbed for hunter seat equitation in the 1970s), jumping position was referred to as the "two-point" seat. The upper body is angled forward, the hips are back, and the seat is slightly out of the saddle (just the cloth of the breeches touching). The weight of the seat transfers to the two thighs, which rest on (rather than grip) the flaps of the saddle—hence the name "two-point." For me, the positions now called the "forward seat," "forward position," and "jumping position" are the same as the two-point seat.

What I called the "three-point seat" is now known as the "full seat," where the rider is upright with her seat in the saddle and her weight distributed over three points of contact: the seat and the flat areas of the two thighs against the saddle.

The "light seat" where the body is inclined slightly forward, is in between the two- and three-point seats. The rider transfers some of the weight from the seat to the thighs, but not all. Generally, the light seat is ridden with longer stirrups, which prevents the rider from getting completely forward out of the saddle.

Notice what happens when you go into a light seat or forward position. Do you feel unstable? Do you have to grip with your knees or hang onto the reins for balance? Are your legs braced? Can your horse pull you out of the saddle? Place one hand on your lower back. Go from a full (three-point) seat to a forward (two-point) seat several times to feel if your back is flat, rounded, or hollowed. Where do you fold? Your back needs to remain flat while you fold at your hips for a solid, forward seat.

EXERCISE

On the Ground and On the Horse

Practice this exercise off the horse first by sitting on a level surface like a mounting block or bench. Once you have the feeling of folding at the hips with a flat back, mount up.

Standing still, hold your reins in one hand, make a fist with this hand, and press it into your horse's neck just above the withers. Place your other hand on your thigh, palm down, and rest as much of your forearm on your thigh as possible. If you have long arms, you may end up with your hand near your knee (fig. 18.1) You might notice that your back is slightly curved to the side. This is fine, and will not cause a problem.

In this position, observe the shape of your back. Gently change from rounded to slightly hollowed while keeping your forearm on your thigh (figs. 18.2 A & B). If you feel any pain, stop, or make smaller movements and go slower. As you continue notice what happens to your pelvis, hips, and head. Sense how your head and pelvis follow the shape of the spine (see Fix 7, p. 27, a similar exercise done with your hands behind you on the horse's back). After a while, look for the *middle* between hollowing and rounding. Here, you will be able lengthen your spine from pelvis to head, which is not possible when you are hollowed or rounded. As you lengthen—a small move—your hips will sink back toward the cantle and the top of your head will move forward and up away from your seat. Slowly sit upright, let your forearm come away from your thigh, and again sense the length of your spine (fig. 18.3).

Reverse your hand positions and repeat the exercise on the other side. After you have found the *middle* again on both sides, see if you can incline slightly forward into a light seat, while keeping the length of your back so that you fold only at your hips. You don't need to incline very far forward. Increase the amount of fold until you are in a forward position. (You may need to shorten your stirrups for this.) The amount you fold forward is dependent on what you are jumping. When you are going over a log on the ground, only a slightly forward incline is necessary; when jumping a 3-foot fence, you will need to incline forward a bit more.

18.1   The rider has folded forward from her hips. Notice the length in her back. She is over her feet with her hips well back.

18.2 A & B   The rider has rounded her back and folded forward at the waist in A. Her weight is on the horse's shoulders and her head is dropping forward and down. Notice the tension in her rein arm. In B, the rider has inclined forward by hollowing her back. Her weight has gone forward onto the horse's shoulders, and this action will put him on his forehand.

18.3   The rider has opened at the hips to sit upright. She has maintained the length in her back, which allows her hips to move freely and easily. Her head is balanced over her seat.

19 Find Your Hips for a Solid Forward Position

Caution
Be careful when first reaching for your horse's ears. Have someone at his head to check his reaction and reach forward slowly. If the saddle doesn't fit he may feel pain as your weight shifts forward, and if you surprise him, he might raise his head abruptly and hit you in the face. Lower your head along the side of his neck to avoid being injured.

Stop
End the exercise if your horse is anxious or uncomfortable, or won't stand still.

Use this 5-Minute Fix to learn to fold at your hip joints. In the forward position, regardless of the degree of angle, folding at your hips ensures that you remain deep and secure in the saddle. When riding on the flat, mobility in your hips allows you to absorb the motion of your horse, helping you sit the trot more easily.

Do you:

- **Feel stiff in your hips?**
- **Have difficulty folding at the hips for a light, or forward (two-point) seat?**
- **Have trouble sitting the trot?**

The ability to move at the hips rather than the waist is important for an effective seat and a solid overall position. Here's a quick tip to improve your awareness of your hips.

Have you ever noticed when you jump that you either get pitched forward as the horse goes over the fence or you fall back in the saddle on landing? Do you, perhaps, feel as if one or both hips are stiff whenever you ride? The problem may not be in your hips but instead in the way you use your pelvis in relation to your hips.

Your hips are ball-and-socket joints. If there were no ligaments (fibrous tissue that connects bone to bone) and muscles in the way, you would be able to put both of your feet behind your head because of the design of these joints. There are five strong ligaments that prevent the hip joint from going too far in one direction or the other. These ligaments act to control hip joint movement without the use of muscles. (Of course, there are some people who are flexible enough to put their feet behind their head, regardless.)

The *iliofemoral* (pelvis-femur) ligament is the strongest ligament in the human body. This triangular or inverted Y-shaped band extends from the pelvis to the femur (thigh bone) in front of the hip joint. When standing, this ligament is under tension, thus preventing the torso from falling backward. When sitting, the tension decreases, permitting the pelvis to tilt backward and allowing increased mobility in the hip joint.

Translated into riding, when the pelvis and lower back are in a "standing" posture in the saddle—that is, when you ride with a *hollowed* back—the *iliofemoral* ligament is under tension, which pulls the ball tighter into the socket and limits range of motion in the hip joint. But, when you ride with a *flattened* back, the pelvis tilts slightly backward into a sitting position and the ligament is no longer under tension, allowing you greater freedom of movement in the hip joint.

In addition to ligaments, there are muscles that surround the hip joint to move the leg in various directions: *adduction* (toward the midline); *abduction* (away from the midline); *internal rotation* (knee in); *external rotation* (knee out); *extending the hip* (opening the hip angle or moving the leg away from the body); and *flexing the hip joint* (closing the hip angle or bringing the leg toward the body).

In most cases, it is the position of the pelvis and lower back that creates the feeling of having stiff hips, not a physical limitation in the actual joint. If you can stand up and sit down without pain, then usually it is how you use yourself in the saddle that is the cause of your stiff-feeling hips.

EXERCISE

On the Horse

To improve awareness of the hips and how much they can move, try this exercise mounted. (You can also do this lesson unmounted, but note that sitting in the saddle does make a big difference.) On a quiet horse, fold forward and see if you can touch your horse's ears. Notice whether your arms feel too short—the result of your back being *hollowed* (fig 19.1). Or, whether you feel as if you are falling onto the horse's neck from a *rounded* back (fig. 19.2). Or, perhaps you are staying well balanced over your feet as a result of a *flat* back (fig. 19.3).

Take one hand and feel your back. Is it hollowed, rounded, or flattened? Place your hands on each side of the horse's neck and slowly change the angle of your pelvis from forward and down (*anterior tilt*) to back and down (*posterior tilt*). In which position is it the easiest for you to close your hips and reach your horse's ears?

If you feel as if you can't find a good position no matter what you do, push your buttocks toward the cantle of the saddle. This gives you a bit more room to fold at the hips rather than the waist. Let yourself rest onto the saddle as you fold down. Explore your position. Notice that when you fold at the hips your arms extend without effort.

When your back is *hollow*, you will not be able extend your arms easily and will have to pull yourself up with your upper back to return to the full seat because your hips can't open easily. When your back is *round*, your arms will feel very heavy and want to drop down toward the lower portion of the horse's neck instead of the ears. You will not be able to get close to the horse's neck with your body because your hip angle is too open. When your back is *flat*, you will be able to close and open at the hips like a hinge. You may not be able to touch your horse' ears if your arms are short, but you will be able to extend your arms easily in the attempt.

Practice finding the pelvic alignment that allows your hips to open and close, like a hinge. Slide your hands toward you, still on the top of your horse's neck, and see if you can push yourself upright by opening at the hips while

19.1 The rider has hollowed her back, which has closed the hip angle too much, preventing her from reaching the horse's ears. Her weight is forward on the withers instead of back in the saddle.

19.2 The rider has rounded her back, folding at the waist instead of the hips. This restricts her shoulders and causes her arms to drop down instead of reaching forward.

19.3 A good fold at the hips allows the rider to touch the horse's ears. Notice that her flattened lower back and pelvis are in alignment with her upper back so her arms extend easily.

keeping your back flat and pelvis in line with your back. Do not change the angle of the pelvis when you sit up. Go slowly and sense when the alignment of your pelvis makes the opening and closing at your hips feel simple and smooth. Then go back to your old position and notice the difference.

Arms

Introduction

When teaching a lesson, I always begin by addressing the rider's pelvis first, then I move up and out to the extremities—the arms and legs. Many times, the arms are "unconsciously" trying to assist the rider's balance much like the tightrope walker's balancing pole. Once the torso is well aligned, it is easier to improve a rider's arm position.

Being able to maintain a relaxed arm position is proof that the rider is secure in the seat and supple in the hips. Throughout history, riders wielding a bow and arrow, sword or spear, have attached the reins to their waist for steering, which exemplifies the importance of the seat. The following lessons are designed to help you gain confidence in your newfound seat position and begin to develop independent hands.

20 | Elbows by Your Sides

Use this 5-Minute Fix before you begin to ask your horse to slow down, stop, or go forward. Adjust the reins to your position instead of adjusting your position to the reins.

> **Do you:**
>
> - **Have trouble stopping your horse?**
> - **Pull back on the reins?**
> - **Fall forward when your horse moves off?**

You may be doing too much with your arms and not enough with your seat. Stabilizing your elbows by your sides may help to solve these problems.

Pay attention to your elbows. Do they drift away from your body? Do they go behind you when you use the reins? Do you extend them forward when asking your horse to move forward? Does it feel like your horse doesn't take the contact? Can he pull you out of the saddle?

Comparable Parts: The Elbow Joint

Human

There is one bone in your upper arm—the *humerus*—and two bones in the forearm—the *radius* and the *ulna*. These three bones meet at the elbow. The point of your elbow is the upper end of the ulna (fig. 20.1 A).

The elbow joint opens and closes like a hinge. Allow your right arm to hang by your side and strongly contract your triceps (the muscles on the back of your arm) to open and extend your elbow as much as you possible can. Now, close the elbow by flexing the biceps, bringing your wrist up to your shoulder. A good elbow position for riding is somewhere in the middle, around a 90-degree angle, depending on the position of your horse's head.

The head of the radius is cylindrical and rotates on the end of the humerus. In humans, the relationship between the radius and the ulna allows you to rotate your hand downward (*pronation*) or upward (*supination*—think of making a cup with your hand to eat soup).

Horse

The horse also has elbow joints (fig. 20.1 B). To find your horse's elbow, run your hand down the shoulder blade until you come to the point of the shoulder. This is where the leg appears to connect to the horse. In fig. 20.1 B, notice the crease that forms in front of the leg where the upper arm (humerus) meets the forearm. Then, follow the upper arm back to the point of the elbow, which is just in front of the horse's girth line. Notice that, unlike ours, the horse's elbow is very close to his body.

The ulna forms the point of the horse's elbow the same as yours; however, here is where horse and human anatomy differs. The radius is the primary weight-bearing bone in the horse's forearm. In the adult horse, the ulna is fused with the radius forming a single bone, which is a good thing! Can you imagine if the horse could rotate his leg between his elbow and knee? I doubt we would be able to ride horses if that could happen.

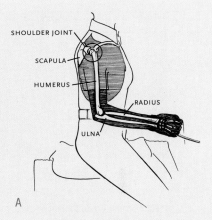

A

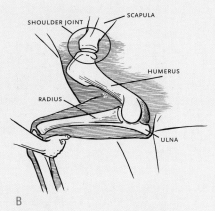

B

20.1 A & B   In the human, the elbow joint is where the humerus and the two bones in the forearm—the ulna and radius—come together (A). The horse's elbow joint features the ulna, which blends into the radius, forming one bone in the forearm (B).

20.2 The correct elbow position. The elbows are slightly in front of the rider's pelvis. This helps to create an elastic feel on the reins.

20.3 The rider's elbows are too straight and her hands are too far in front of the pommel.

20.4 The rider's elbows are too far back. Her hands are almost touching her body and her back has hollowed and stiffened.

Exercise

On the Horse

A good position for your elbows when riding on the flat is just in front of the top of your pelvis (fig. 20.2). This will vary slightly depending on your conformation. A rider with a long waist and short upper arms may find the elbows well above her pelvis, while a short-waisted, long upper-armed rider may have the elbows touching the pelvis. Obviously, there is going to be some movement in the elbows as you follow the horse's mouth, but you want to avoid extremes especially if your horse decides to pull on you (see Fix 24, p. 94).

Your body tends to tip forward when your elbows get too far out in front, which puts the horse on the forehand (fig. 20.3). You can easily get pulled out of the saddle in this position. On the other hand, when you draw your elbows behind your back, you are limited as to how far you can go (fig. 20.4). If you still have not made contact with the horse's mouth, you will likely brace against your stirrups and lean back to get to his mouth (for a quick way to shorten the reins, see Fix 25, p. 98).

Whenever you retract your elbows you are, without question, *pulling*. This is not an issue of finesse but mechanics. Pulling back may cause the horse to open his mouth and/or throw his head in the air, especially when combined with your bracing against the stirrups.

Keep your elbows by your sides. Allow them to move forward and then return to your sides as you follow the horse's movement. Only move your hands forward an inch or two to invite your horse to stretch down, especially if he has a habit of jerking on the reins. You can always lengthen the reins if he wants to stretch deeper. Shorten your reins before you ask for a halt, thus keeping your elbows by your sides when you stop so that you can use your seat more effectively.

Elbow Position for Optimum Shoulder Comfort

Use this 5-Minute Fix to find a relaxed, comfortable upper-arm position. Decreasing any tension in your shoulders will help you better communicate with the horse.

Do you:

- **Have trouble steering your horse?**

- **Have a horse that throws up his head when you use the reins?**

- **Think your shoulders feel "stuck" or "jammed"?**

- **Feel like your upper body tips forward, or your back hollows, even though you try to stay in good alignment?**

The source of your problems may be how you use your arms to communicate with your horse.

Next time you ride, notice where you carry your hands. Do you have them close together in front of your stomach or are they wide apart? Is one arm held away from your side and/or the other pinched in? When you turn, do you take your elbow away from your body or in across your body?

Carrying your elbows too wide or too narrow can cause tension and create an unstable riding position. Experiment by taking your elbows even further

Comparable Parts: The Shoulder Joint

Human

Your upper arm (the *humerus*) meets your shoulder blade (*scapula*) at a very shallow socket joint (see figs. 20.1 A and 22.1, pp. 83 and 89). The socket is part of the shoulder blade and is much smaller than your hip joint (also a ball and socket joint), meaning there is less of a cup. The top end of the humerus forms what looks like half a ball on a stick. This shallow cup and half-ball arrangement works very well when you need to reach for something—or lead your horse. However, it is not very stable and a lot of ligaments and muscles are required to keep the joint together. Holding your elbows out wide—or in narrow—requires more muscular effort than when you let the upper arms hang down in line with gravity (for more anatomy of the shoulder girdle, see Fix 22, p. 88).

Horse

Horses have a similar arrangement where the shoulder blade and upper arm meet. There is one major difference, however (see fig. 20.1 B, p.83). The horse's socket is much more distinct and restricts movement in the shoulder joint primarily to a forward and backward swing of the limb. Imagine if a horse could raise his leg out to the side the way we do with our arm. This would make the horse very unstable—and most likely unrideable—because he might wind up doing splits with his front legs!

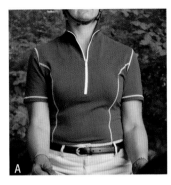  

21.1 A–C   A good upper arm position is shown in A. The rider has let her upper arms hang from the shoulder joints. The elbows are softly by her sides and her hands are about shoulder-width apart. She is relaxed in the shoulders and able to follow the motion of the horse's head with her hands. In B, the elbows are too wide. This requires more effort from her shoulders and stiffens her arms, thus preventing her from following the motion of the horse's head. In C, the rider has pulled her elbows in, pinching her arms to her sides. This restricts movement in her seat and makes her less secure in the saddle because of the tension in her shoulders.

away and then bringing them closer together to feel what happens in your neck, upper back, and shoulders. Both of these positions require extra muscular effort.

EXERCISE

On the Horse

To find a relaxed position for your upper arm, let gravity help you. Allow your arms to hang straight down. Then, simply bend at the elbow to raise your hands in front of you for holding the reins. Your body conformation will determine exactly where your elbows touch your sides (see Fix 20, p. 82). This place will be comfortable and take little effort (figs. 21.1 A–C).

If you need more stability—for example, your horse is trying to pull you out of the saddle—"Velcro" or hug your upper arm to your rib cage so you don't get tense in the shoulders. This makes you more secure because you have functionally shortened the lever between your arms and your seat. Remember, the longer a lever, the less force you need to move something. With your elbows "hugged" it is as if the reins were attached to your pelvis, bypassing your upper body. This decreases tension in the reins, which your horse feels in his mouth, because your shoulders can't get involved.

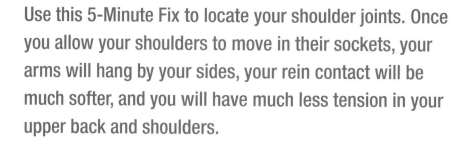

22 | Finding Your Shoulder Joints

Use this 5-Minute Fix to locate your shoulder joints. Once you allow your shoulders to move in their sockets, your arms will hang by your sides, your rein contact will be much softer, and you will have much less tension in your upper back and shoulders.

Do you:

- **Find your shoulders get stiff when you ride?**

- **Have a hard time following the bit?**

- **Feel like your horse can pull you out of the saddle any time he wants to?**

- **Pull your shoulders up to your ears and hold your breath when asking the horse to stop?**

Here's a quick tip to help you resolve many of your shoulder issues with a simple understanding of anatomy.

Next time you ride, notice what you do with your shoulders. Are they drawn up, back, or down? Is one higher than the other? Do you have a limited range of motion in one shoulder? Are they sore after you ride? Do you know where the joints are, or do you simply refer to the general area as "the shoulder"? Riders often have a vague notion of their shoulders, but the shoulder joints can become restricted by this lack of clarity and interfere with their horse's mouth.

Shoulders are defined as the part of the body between the neck and upper arm, or as the joint connecting the arm with the torso. Anatomically, these two definitions are very different! To improve your shoulder position and rein contact you need to understand the shoulder area's anatomy.

The shoulder girdle is comprised of the collarbone (*clavicle*) and shoulder blade (*scapula*). This not really a "girdle" because by definition, a girdle is an encircling or ring-like structure: the collarbones connect to the manubrium portion of the sternum, but the shoulder blades do not touch each other at the back, so there really isn't an encircling ring (see Fix 6, p. 22). Instead, when looked at from the side, the collarbone and shoulder blade form a "V" shape, which rests on the rib cage (see fig. 20.1 A, p. 83). The first rib lies directly underneath this "V."

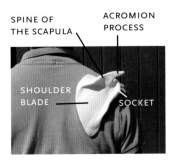

22.1   The shoulder blade from behind.

EXERCISE

On the Ground

To find your shoulder socket start by tracing along the outside edge of the shoulder blade (fig. 22.1). As you follow this outside edge up into the armpit you may be able to feel the edge of the socket, though if you have a lot of muscle in this area, it may be difficult. The socket is part of the shoulder blade, below another part called the *acromion process*, which forms from the spine of the shoulder blade. I call this a "ledge" because it is like an overhang keeping the socket safe beneath it. When you put your hand on the top of your shoulder, you are touching the acromion process.

To get a sense of the shoulder joint, place the palm of your hand in your armpit and gently grasp your upper arm from underneath (fig. 22.2). Move your arm so that you can feel the ball moving in the socket. Notice how much lower the actual joint is from the top of the shoulder area! When you tense the muscles above this joint by pulling your shoulders up, movement is severely restricted in this ball and socket joint.

22.2   To locate your shoulder joint, place the palm of your hand in your armpit and gently grasp the top of your upper arm from underneath. Move your arm around to feel the ball moving in the socket.

22.3 A & B   This rider is very tense in her shoulders. Notice how they are drawn up toward her ears (A). When the rider's shoulder girdle rests on the rib cage and her shoulder joints are free to move, it allows her to follow the horse's mouth (B).

In order to have good contact with the reins and a comfortable, solid arm position, you need to allow the shoulder ball-and-socket joints to have movement just like your hips (see Fix 19, p. 76). You can practice letting the upper arms "hang" from the shoulder sockets when you are driving your car or pushing a grocery store cart.

On the Horse

Next time you are mounted, gently grasp your armpit area to identify the edge of the shoulder socket, as well as the ball moving in the socket. Do this on both sides. Remind yourself of their location as you ride. Notice how—when you do this—your elbows sink and your horse relaxes into the contact. Then, go back to your old shoulder habits and feel what happens. Observe the quality of your contact and your horse's reaction to the bit.

Recognizing the location of your shoulder joints when you are holding the reins eliminates unnecessary tension in the shoulder area. Your contact becomes much softer and more pleasant to your horse (figs. 22.3 A & B).

Connecting Your Elbows

Use this 5-Minute Fix as a body position self-check to remind you to keep your elbows where they belong. As your seat improves you will no longer notice the bandage's presence.

Training Aid
Ace® bandage

Caution
Test the stretch of the Ace bandage with your elbows before wearing it while mounted. It is important you recognize that the bandage is only to serve as a reminder and that it is not there to restrict your arms.

Stop
If the Ace bandage makes you feel panicky or trapped, discontinue the exercise. Do not wear the bandage when riding over fences.

Do you:

- **Have trouble keeping your elbows by your sides?**

- **Find they both tend to drift out of control? Or perhaps you have one wayward elbow?**

The solution to elbows that stick out like chicken wings may be having a tactile sense of them by your sides so that you can discover the benefits of this position.

Pay attention to your elbows. Observe how close they are to your sides (fig. 23.1). Is there a large gap under both or just one elbow? Do they stick out to the sides over a jump? Experiment by riding with your elbows further away from your body. How does this affect you and your horse? Then find out what happens when you clamp your elbows against your sides. Feel how either can make you unbalanced and stiff.

23.1 **This rider's elbows unconsciously drift away from her sides.**

Often, an elbow problem has more to do with your seat than your arms. When your hips are stiff, your elbows may widen in an effort to increase your stability. Where only one elbow sneaks away it may be a result of collapsing on one side of your rib cage (see Fixes 8 and 9, pp. 31 and 35). Whatever the cause, a simple Ace bandage may help.

EXERCISE

On the Horse

Find a 2- or 3-inch-wide Ace bandage, preferably one that still has good stretch to it. Get an assistant to help you before mounting. Have her wrap the bandage around your arms just above your elbows while they are resting by your sides. You may need to have it wrapped around twice. It should be comfortably snug (not taut), and fastened with a bow knot (fig. 23.2).

In order to mount, slide the bandage up to your neck like a necklace (fig. 23.3). Once on your horse you can move it back into position just above your elbows (fig. 23.4). When you finish your ride, simply slide the bandage up around your neck and over your head (take your helmet off first) to remove it. This saves having to find someone to tie it for you each time you ride. Next time, simply slip the looped bandage over your head and you are ready to go.

You want the bandage to act as a physical reminder when your elbows start to drift. Should you get into trouble, you can still use your arms because *the Ace bandage will stretch*. It is important to realize this ahead of time so test that the bandage will "give" by taking your elbows away from your body (fig. 23.5).

Once mounted start at the walk. (Note: if you are extremely uncomfortable, *take the bandage off right away* and try this lesson again later.) Even though it may feel awkward, continue your ride as usual. Notice what changes in your seat, arms, and hands when you are physically reminded to keep your elbows in. When you no longer notice the bandage, take it off; use it weekly as a tune-up until you can maintain your elbows by your sides.

23.2   Have an assistant tie the Ace bandage to the correct length around you.

23.3   Move the bandage up around your neck like a necklace prior to mounting.

23.4   The rider with the Ace bandage adjusted down around her arms while mounted. The bandage is snug but not tight, so she only feels it when her elbows try to drift away.

23.5   Even though the bandage reminds the rider to keep her elbows in, it is stretchy enough so she can easily move her arms, if necessary.

24 Stop Pulling on Your Horse

Use this 5-Minute Fix as a body-position self-check whenever you want to establish a frame between your seat and hands. Go through the steps before taking up your reins, then shorten your reins to your adjusted body position, rather than altering your position to take up the slack in the reins.

Do you:

- Pull on your horse's mouth even though you know you shouldn't?

- Hear your instructor tell you to "give to your horse," but you are not sure how?

- Try to "throw away" the reins after you have used them in an attempt to stop yourself from pulling, only to then lose your balance?

It can be difficult to take a contact on your horse's mouth without pulling. Whether through the reins and bit, or a rope halter and lead, you need to communicate with your horse. But, how can you use your reins kindly, yet firmly? Here's a quick tip to help you stop pulling, start "giving" (even when you have contact), and improve overall communication.

The next time you ride, notice what you do when you ask your horse to move off, slow down, or stop. Do you hollow or do you round your back? Do your hands get closer to your body? Do your elbows go behind you? If the distance from your hands to your body decreases when you use your reins, you are pulling on your horse's mouth.

Often, riders inadvertently grab on the reins to catch their balance. Others have been taught to pull back to stop or slow down. Many try to solve the problem of pulling back by throwing their hands forward immediately afterward. But, a sudden release like this can disturb the horse's balance, causing him to trip or stumble. This is sometimes seen when a rider approaching a fence drops the horse just before takeoff, causing a refusal or a rough, abrupt takeoff instead of a smooth, efficient jump.

A good rider rides seat-to-hands because she has a stable body position providing the necessary support to guide the horse through the seat to the hands without pulling back. This is established with the correct position of the lower back (see Fix 10, p. 42). While, simply stabilizing the lower back may be enough to communicate with a sensitive horse, there will be times when it is necessary to use the reins. It is necessary to learn how to maintain a "frame" between your body and your hands, leaving the wither area in front of the pommel open.

When you are in a correct full-seat frame, a vertical line can be drawn through your ear, shoulder, and hip. Your upper arms hang by your sides (see Fixes 21 and 22, pp. 85 and 88), your elbows are bent, and your forearms lengthen forward to the hands without weighing on the horse's mouth (see Fixes 19 and 27, pp. 76 and 104). When you learn to maintain this frame and shorten the reins to your position, you will stop pulling on your horse even when you have a firm contact in your hands.

EXERCISE

On the Ground

Off the horse, you can practice this exercise in a narrow doorway. Stand in the doorway with your back against one side and your knees bent. Place your fists against the other side of the doorway and press your back and fists into the opposing sides. Feel the space created between your body and your fists. In the saddle, this area would be the wither area in front of the pommel.

Now imagine holding the reins while maintaining this frame. Close your fingers as if to communicate with the bit while keeping your fists solidly pressed against the doorway. If your tendency is to pull back when you close your hands, your fists will no longer stay against the door frame; if you were riding, you would be pulling on your horse's mouth. Practice keeping your fists against the opposing door frame as you slightly open and close your fingers so that you learn how to keep pressing your hands forward even when you increase the contact with your horse's mouth.

On the Horse

To find your solid frame, have an assistant press against your lower back with one hand, and against your soft fist in front of you with her other hand (figs. 24.1 A & B) Maintain your elbows by your sides. Make small changes in your lower back and pelvis until you find a solid position (see Fixes 10, 12, and 13, pp. 42, 51, and 55). Make the forward pressure with your hand equal to your back pressure; you won't need to do too much when your body is stable and correct, even if she presses firmly.

Be careful not to break the line through the wrist downward or upward to temporarily shorten the reins. This is still in effect pulling back and often causes the rider to round in the shoulders (see Fix 45, p. 173, for a way to straighten your wrists). Be sure to press evenly across all the knuckles. This connects you through the underside of the forearm, back of the upper arm, and down your back to your helper's other hand, which deepens your seat.

Now find out what happens if you hollow, then round your back: your assistant will be able to push your fist back easily, or at least, you will need

24.1 A & B   The rider is able to relax and easily resist the pressure on her back and fist because her back is flat, therefore stable, as she presses toward my hands (A). Keep the forearm parallel to the ground with the fist softly closed as if you were going to punch a wall, and make sure that you are pressing across all the knuckles, including the pinky finger (B).

to use a lot more arm and shoulder strength to resist her pressure (figs. 24.2 A & B). Reestablish your solid frame and slightly close and open your fingers on the reins without moving your hand away from your helper's.

Finally, go for a ride and imagine that your assistant's hands are still there. If you need to use the reins, shorten them to your position in order to maintain your frame. This prevents you from pulling your hands back to make contact with your horse's mouth, thereby allowing you to ride "seat-to-hand" instead of "hand-to-seat."

24.2 A & B   The rider has hollowed her back and is no longer able to resist my pressure on her fist (A). As a result, I can push her arm backward. If she were holding the reins, she would pull on the horse's mouth because she can't maintain her arm position and balance. When the rider rounds her back, again, her elbow goes back, and she is unable to resist me when I push on her hand (B).

25 Shorten Your Reins without Pulling on Your Horse's Mouth

Use this 5-Minute Fix to help you quickly shorten your reins without pulling back. Practice until you can do it without fumbling so you can use this technique—automatically—when you most need it.

> **Do you:**
> - Scramble to shorten your reins?
> - Pitch forward when you do so?
> - Find your horse throws his head up as a result?

There are a number of circumstances where being able to quickly and smoothly shorten your reins is necessary. For instance, during a dressage test after the free walk; after a jump if you had to slip your reins; or if your horse startles on the trail. You want to be efficient, without disturbing your horse.

Exercise

On the Ground and On the Horse

Here is a three-step process to shorten your reins quickly, efficiently, and without pulling on your horse's mouth:

1   Take the bight (the loop or end of the rein) in one hand. Firmly grasp both reins with the other hand and press your fist against the horse's neck. This prevents you from pulling on the horse's mouth (fig. 25.1).

2   Draw back on the bight by moving your arm diagonally away from the fist hand (fig. 25.2). You are limited as to how much you can shorten the reins if the bight hand comes directly toward you. Make sure the fist hand remains firmly pressed into the horse's neck. How much draw will determine how short you make the reins. The action of shortening the reins comes from your arm, not your hand.

3   Drop the bight and separate the reins into your two hands (fig. 25.3). When you draw the bight with your right hand, you take up the right rein. When you draw the bight with your left hand, take up the left rein. Keep pushing on the horse's neck until you have separated the reins into your two hands (fig. 25.4). This is a very solid position and prevents you from getting ripped out of the saddle should the horse pull on the reins or stumble. This is especially useful after a jump. Once the horse has accepted the contact, you can lift your hands off his neck.

Practice this three-step method off the horse, then, on your horse while standing still, and finally in motion at all gaits. When practicing, it is not important how much you draw the bight to shorten the reins—you only need to draw the slack out of the reins. It is important you develop good technique. Then, when you actually need to shorten your reins quickly, your practice will pay off. Remember to switch hands so you can shorten your reins both right- and left-handed.

25.1   I take the bight of the rein in my left hand.

25.2   I draw my left hand up, which is holding the bight, by taking my elbow back at an angle away from my body (like drawing a bow), thereby shortening the reins. Notice that I continue to press my right fist into the horse's neck. This keeps me from pitching forward and/or pulling on the reins.

25.3   I drop the bight and take the left rein with my left hand while maintaining the pressure of my right fist on the horse's neck.

25.4   Now, I take the reins in two hands, and my fists are securely pressing into the horse's neck.

26 | Combing the Reins

Use this 5-Minute Fix to improve contact with your horse's mouth. Once you have learned how to do this exercise, "combing" the reins will serve as a good warm-up. You can "comb out" tension and resistance in you and your horse.

Caution
Be aware of the outside rein during this exercise: when your reins are long, it may drop down. Hold a loop of rein in your outside hand to prevent your horse from catching his front leg in it.

Do you:

- Have a horse that travels with his head in the air? Or throws it up as soon as you touch the reins?

- Find he is "allergic" to the bit?

- Try to pull his head down without success?

- Have problems with a "stretchy" circle in your dressage test because your horse won't reach down to the bit?

Here's a simple exercise to improve your horse's contact with the bit.

Next time you ride notice what happens when you ask your horse to take the bit. Does he resist or hollow his back? Does he jerk hard against the reins? Is his neck like concrete? And how do you react? Do you pull back sharply, stiffen or brace against your horse's mouth, or simply let him travel with his head in the air, with occasional attempts to "saw" it down by pulling on alternate reins?

Both you and your horse play a role in good contact—that is, the horse is relaxed in his mouth and accepts the contact of your hands through the reins. A horse that drops behind the bit or one that leans on the bit is not meeting the bit correctly. If your hands are unsteady or you use your horse's mouth for balance, he is not likely to accept your contact. Both you and the horse need to meet the bit softly and firmly for good contact.

EXERCISE

On the Horse

You can learn how to establish a friendly relationship with your horse's mouth by "combing" the reins. While mounted in an enclosed arena, begin at a standstill. Take the inside rein, and "comb" it with your two hands in a way similar to the overhand motion of pulling in a rope (fig. 26.1). Use a palm-up position so that you don't round your shoulders (fig. 26.2). "Let go" in your shoulders and allow the rein to slide through your hands as you do this slow, smooth, and rhythmical hand-over-hand motion (see also Fix 22, p. 88).

Try not to bend your horse's head around to the side. Instead, you should just be able to see his inside eye and have him stretch down into the rein. Can you continuously comb the rein without grabbing, holding your breath, or stopping the motion? Now repeat the exercise with the other rein.

After practicing at the halt, have your horse walk. Often the forward motion helps him get the idea of lengthening his neck down into the contact. Don't worry too much about steering at first. It is more important to keep your horse moving, as this will improve both the contact and steering.

If he puts his head in the air, take the slack out of the inside rein by reaching further up toward the bit with your hands and continue combing (fig. 26.3). If he puts his head down, let the reins slide through your hands and stop combing (fig. 26.4). This makes it very clear that you would like him to put his head down instead of up. Meanwhile, notice if you feel as if you want to "grab" whenever your horse changes his head position or speed. This action may be the actual cause of your contact problem.

26.1   Combing the inside left rein, correctly, with my palm up.

26.2   Turning the palm down causes my shoulder to round forward, which puts more weight on the horse's forehand.

26.3   To shorten the rein, reach further down toward the bit with your inside hand. As you draw your hand back, do not give as much rein to the horse and continue combing. Notice that my hand is in a palm-up position as I reach further down, which keeps my shoulder open.

26.4   Lengthen the rein by allowing it to slide through your hands as the horse reaches down toward the bit.

Once your horse lengthens down at the walk in both directions, begin combing one rein at the trot. Go his easy way (the direction in which he is more responsive) first, and continue in this direction until you can get him to lengthen down into that rein. Regulate his speed with your rising, and if necessary, use the outside rein.

When your horse remains stretched down at the trot, add transitions from walk to trot and back to walk while combing the rein. Can you maintain the lengthened neck position throughout the transitions while combing continuously? Return to walk and change direction.

Again, trot while combing the rein. If you stop combing as you make changes of gait or transitions, you are tensing and your contact will be harsh or inconsistent. Continue the exercise until you can comb uninterrupted through the transitions.

Next, change direction while combing and trotting. You will need to change to the new inside rein as you pass from one direction to the other. Allow the outside rein to rest on the horse's neck but be careful it doesn't droop down around his legs. If this happens, pick up a loop of rein and hold it in your outside hand as you continue to comb the inside rein.

Practice until the changeover becomes smooth. Once the horse is relaxed into the contact in both directions, take the reins in two hands but still allow him to stretch down. When it comes time to shorten his frame, simply stop letting the reins slide through your hands. If you have done this exercise well, your horse will now accept the contact (see Fix 24, p. 94, for finding your own frame).

27 Unstick Your Elbows

●●●●●●

Use this 5-Minute Fix to improve your balance and the suppleness of your elbows when you ride. This exercise is an excellent way to develop "independent hands" over fences.

Training Aids
Stick, short whip, or
dowel, tilt board

Caution
Be careful when using
a tilt board. Familiarize
yourself with one before
you start using one with
the stick. Use of your
hands is very limited in
this lesson.

Stop
If your horse becomes
nervous, stop and let
go of the stick so that
you can use your
hands freely.

Do you:

- **Tend to grab at the reins?**

- **Have a hard time "giving" to your horse, especially over a jump?**

- **Want to lock your elbows?**

- **Find your horse "complains" about your contact?**

Here's a quick tip to "unstick" your elbows by using a little crop or short dowel.

Next time you ride, notice what happens to your elbows. Do they go behind your body? Do you want to pin them to your sides? Are you afraid to let your arms go forward, following your horse's mouth over a jump?

As I said in Fix 20, (p. 82), your elbows are hinge joints. They need to open and close with the horse's movement. When you hold your elbows in a fixed position, it makes your hands go up and down, bumping the horse in the mouth. In this lesson you will learn to find your balance independently from your arms.

EXERCISE

On the Ground

You need a short stick: a riding crop will do, or a thin dowel. Start on the ground, standing with your knees slightly bent. Hold the stick on top of your index fingers and under your thumbs, with your hands in riding position as if you were holding the reins (fig. 27.1). Practice extending your arms until they are straight. It might help to think of pushing the stick away from you. Be sure to bend your knees as you extend your arms so that you can maintain your balance.

27.1 **Hold the stick under your thumbs and on top of your index fingers.**

Increase the difficulty of this exercise by standing on a tilt board. A board that only tilts forward and back is easier than the round-bottomed disks. To start, place the board near a wall for support, or have a friend "spot" you. Stand with your feet hip-width apart on the board (fig. 27.2). Keep the board *slightly* tilted back but do not let either end touch the ground. Flatten your back and let your weight sink into your heels (fig. 27.3). Then, extend your arms fully while maintaining your balance. Return your arms to your sides and extend again several times without allowing the tilt board to move. Next, fold into a jumping position, keeping the board still and again, extend your arms (figs. 27.4 A & B). Do this one a little at a time as you might discover your quads are not fit enough for extended periods on the board, and you may put too much weight in your toes or your heels (27.5 A & B).

On the Horse

Once mounted, place the stick under your thumbs again while holding the reins. At the halt, extend your arms and make sure that your horse is okay with this idea (fig. 27.6). Some horses worry about the stick or get nervous when the rider's hands extend over their neck. Do not continue with this part of the exercise if your horse becomes anxious. Instead, spend some time getting him accustomed to the stick over his neck—for example, only moving one hand forward at a time.

27.3   On the board, I start by extending and bending my elbows while in a full seat—upright dressage position—keeping the board level.

27.2   Use a tilt board to practice balance. You can purchase one on the internet or from a fitness store, or make one with a small round piece of wood and a short, wide plank (this type is less stable so be careful). Extend and bend your elbows several times without allowing the tilt board to move or touch the ground.

27.4 A & B   I fold into the forward seat with the stick extended out in front of me (A). Closing my angles even further tests my ability to stay in balance at different stirrup lengths (B).

In A, I have too much weight on the front of my feet. My knees are straight and I stiffen to keep from falling forward. Too much weight in my heels causes me to fall back, in B. I have thrown my upper body forward to compensate.

27.6 While holding the stick level, extend both hands over the horse's neck. You can shorten your reins as necessary in this position.

Once your horse accepts the idea, begin to walk. Time the forward movement of the stick in rhythm with your horse's movement. Don't rush the stick! See if you can ride to a halt while keeping the stick extended in front of you. It is okay to shorten your reins—a lot in some cases. Then, proceed at the trot and eventually the canter.

You may want to shorten your stirrups a hole or two if you are used to riding long so that you remain balanced as you extend your arms. Experiment with keeping your arms fully extended in the full seat—that is, upright—and again in a forward seat (fig. 27.7 and see Fix 18, p. 72). This is a great way to check your balance in preparation for an automatic release—maintaining a straight line from elbow to bit—over fences. See if you can keep the stick steady and fully extended over poles or cross-rails.

27.7 Fold forward into a forward seat while keeping the stick level and extended in front of you.

Legs

Introduction

A solid leg position is essential to a good seat. When I taught in Italy there was no translation for the word "seat." There was only a word used to describe the rider's "fork": the seat and thighs combined, meaning that the thigh is considered *part* of the seat. Therefore, good thigh contact is essential for your stability. Thigh contact also helps distribute your weight around the horse's rib cage, which alleviates some of the pressure on his back.

The function of the stirrups is to provide you with a solid base of support, like standing on the ground. While all of the lessons are helpful, perhaps my favorite one in this section is Fix 34 on p. 135, Mirror, Mirror on the Wall. This lesson shows you just how powerful your self-image is!

Review the Guidelines to Learning before you begin this section (p. xiv).

28 A Quick Measure for Accurate Stirrup Length

Training Aids
Dressage whip, string

Use this 5-Minute Fix to ensure your stirrup leathers are even. This is especially important when riding school horses or when someone else has used your saddle.

Do you:

- **Ever feel as if your stirrups are not even?**

- **Try stepping harder into one stirrup but it doesn't solve the problem?**

- **Stand in front of your horse, or ask someone else to see if your stirrups are the same length?**

Here are a few quick tips that take the guesswork out of determining if your stirrups are even.

Riding with even stirrups is important to help you sense and feel when you are straight in the saddle. Many riders are unaware when their stirrups are uneven. Others know something doesn't "feel right" but aren't sure what it is. Uneven leathers can be the source of feeling crooked, but there can be other causes as well: a crooked saddle, or a horse with one side of his back lower than the other, can give you the impression that the problem is your stirrups.

Start with a quick stirrup length check in order to rule it out as the source of the issue. If, after measuring your stirrups the feeling persists, you might want to investigate other possibilities (see Fix 15, p. 63).

EXERCISE

On the Ground

The most common way to check your stirrups is to stand in front of the horse with the saddle on and try to eye them to see if they are hanging at the same height. Unfortunately, your eye might not give you accurate information. When your horse is standing crookedly or is on unlevel ground, the level of the stirrups could appear to be uneven when in fact, they are the same. It is best to literally *measure* your stirrups for accuracy.

With an English saddle, the fastest way to measure stirrup length is to "roll" or turn the stirrup up, measuring the distance from the tread of the stirrup to the bottom of the saddle flap (fig. 28.1). You may have a little bit of leather showing or the tread may be slightly above the bottom of the flap. Go around to the other stirrup and repeat the process comparing the difference. (This method assumes that the saddle flaps are cut to the same length.) If the difference is more than half an inch, take one stirrup up or down depending on the length you prefer.

If the difference is less than half an inch, you might as well leave the stirrups alone. On English leathers, the holes are usually set one inch apart. Given that a stirrup leather is folded in half, raising your stirrup one hole changes the overall length about

28.1   You can measure the stirrup leathers against the flap of the saddle. Roll the stirrup up to see how close the tread comes to the bottom of the flap. Repeat this process on the other side.

28.2 Here I use a piece of string to measure the length of the stirrup. Make sure you keep the string taut and measure from the same place at the top of each leather for accuracy.

half that distance. When unevenness is less than half an inch, you won't be able to resolve the difference unless you punch new holes.

Another method for measuring your leathers is to use string or a stick (fig. 28.2). This is easier than taking them off, which can be quite a difficult job on some saddles—especially when the saddle is girthed up. Take a piece of string—baling twine will do—and place one end at the top of the leather's buckle when it is firmly seated against the stirrup bar. Pull the string tight and mark the distance to the bottom of the stirrup. Walk the string around to the other side and measure this length against the other stirrup leather. Adjust the leathers as needed.

You can also use your dressage whip as the measuring device for this technique (fig. 28.3). Simply place one end of the whip on the stirrup bar and mark the distance to the bottom of the stirrup. Keep your mark as you go to the other side to check its leather.

The *best* way to check your stirrup leathers for evenness is to remove them from the saddle altogether and hold them up against each other (fig. 28.4). This takes a bit longer but provides the most accurate measurement. Often, one leather is slightly longer, which can be caused by always mounting from the left, or because you push more strongly on one stirrup when riding. A good solution is to swap the leathers from left to right every month. This way they stretch more evenly and you can quickly check them against each other when you make the switch. Swapping your leathers is especially important when they are new because leather can stretch quite a lot at first.

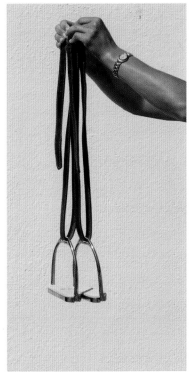

28.3 A dressage whip is another easy tool to measure stirrup length. Be sure to use the same points of reference on each side of the saddle.

28.4 When you swap your leathers each month (a good habit to help counteract the natural stretching of leather), hold them up against each other to see if they are the same length.

If, after checking your stirrups, you still feel uneven, look to see if your horse's back is level and/or if the saddle is twisted (see Fix 15, p. 63). Finally, many people have one leg slightly shorter than the other, but unless you have a significant physical difference, it is best to ride with even stirrups.

29 Level Your Stirrups for a Solid Foundation

Training Aids
Plumb bob, shims or cardboard, Vetrap™, scissors

Use this 5-Minute Fix to establish a solid base of support. Leveling your feet in the saddle will improve your comfort and your ability to communicate with your horse.

Do you:

- **Have trouble keeping your feet flat on the stirrups?**

- **Curl to the outside in an attempt to wrap your leg around the horse?**

- **Jam your boot against the outside branch of the stirrup to find support, yet still feel unstable?**

- **Have ankle and foot pain during or after your ride?**

The answer may be found in your—or your horse's—conformation. "Shimming" your stirrups may resolve these problems.

If you have ever had a pair of ski boots adjusted to your feet, you might remember that the clerk shimmed your boots, also called "canting." This adjustment compensates for your conformation—for example, knock-knees or bowed legs—and any length differences between your two legs. The result is that the ski lies perfectly flat to the snow and you have maximum stability and support without discomfort.

Riding is similar to skiing in that you want your foot flat on the stirrup. And, just like skiing, individual variations can hamper this feeling and deprive you of a solid foundation. In addition to your conformation, the length of your stirrup leather in relation to the roundness of your horse's barrel may cause your stirrup to be angled, which is less-than-ideal for your foot to rest on.

EXERCISE

On the Ground

First, check your equipment. Place your saddle on the horse—with the stirrups pulled down—and look at each stirrup from the front (figs. 29.1 A & B). Is the tread level—that is, parallel to the ground—or angled? Look at the curve of the horse's barrel in relation to the length of the stirrups. If the stirrups hang above the widest part of his rib cage they may be pushed out at an angle. This effect is exaggerated when you have round thighs or a very round-barreled horse. Hold the stirrup a little away from the horse to see if the tread angle increases.

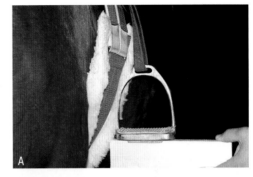

29.1 A & B   A level stirrup (A) and an angled stirrup (B). The board under the angled stirrup is being held parallel to the ground. The stirrup is significantly higher on the outside due to shortening the leather and the roundness of the horse's barrel.

Next, check your conformation by using a "plumb bob"—a weight that is suspended from a string or plumb line and used as a reference perpendicular to the ground. You will need the help of a friend for this. Stand on a level surface and align the plumb line to the center of your kneecap. Have your assistant observe where the bob hangs (figs. 29.2 A–C). It is difficult to look yourself and generally interferes with the test. When the plumb bob is over the second toe, you don't need any shims based on *your* conformation. (You might still need them because of *your horse's* conformation.) If the bob hangs to either side, shim your foot on the outside or inside by using pieces of cardboard until the bob lines up over your second toe.

Carefully take the pieces of cardboard and layer them in the appropriate locations on each stirrup tread. Be sure to twist the stirrup into proper position

29.2 A–C   Use a plumb bob to determine if the center of your kneecap lines up over your second toe (A), to the inside toward your big toe (B), or to the outside toward your little toe (C).

29.3   A standard wedge stirrup pad. I have only used these twice—with riders who had significant conformation issues.

before applying the cardboard and remember which set of cardboard goes where! You may exaggerate the problem by placing the shims incorrectly. Use Vetrap or duct tape to hold the cardboard in place.

The same process can solve the problem when the stirrups are angled as a result of the horse's conformation.

On the Horse

Test ride your stirrups, adding or subtracting cardboard until you find a comfortable amount. You will know when it is right because suddenly your feet will feel flat and you will be more secure in the saddle. You may be thinking at this point that all you need to do is purchase some commercial wedge-shaped stirrup pads (fig. 29.3). I find that this amount of wedge is too extreme, I have only had two students use these pads and one student had to grind the wedge down quite a bit to get to the right amount. If you use the commercial wedge inserts for small changes you take the risk of putting too much strain on your ankles.

A More Permanent Solution

If you find that shimming your stirrups works for you, you may want something a bit better than cardboard. I have created stirrup shims made from material that is several layers of rubber with a leather top (figs. 29.4 A & B). These are available from my website www.murdochmethod.com. The wedge shape is built into the shim so you don't have to mess around with multiple layers of cardboard. You can decrease the angle by peeling away one layer. Note that the wedge generally goes toward the side of the stirrup nearest the horse, especially when the disparity is caused by your horse's round-barreled conformation.

29.4 A & B Easy-to-use Murdoch Method English stirrup shims have a small wedge that works to solve most needs (A). These are easily secured to a stirrup with Vetrap (B).

30 Finding Good Thigh Contact

Use this 5-Minute Fix to find even thigh contact with the saddle. Allowing your thigh to rest on the saddle gives you a better base of support with less muscular effort. It is also more comfortable for your horse because your weight is distributed over a larger surface area.

> **Do you:**
>
> - Have trouble getting your horse to go forward?
>
> - Bump or hit the front of your saddle with your pelvis?
>
> - Grab onto your horse with your calves?
>
> - Feel insecure over fences?
>
> - Find your lower leg swings out of control?

The solution may be establishing good thigh contact with your saddle.

Next time you ride, pay attention to your thighs. Are they close to the saddle, or are your knees turned out? Is there a gap between your knee and the knee roll? Does it feel as if your thighs are being "pushed" out by the saddle or the horse? Do your knees ride forward over the knee roll on the flap? Now, take a moment to assess how well your saddle fits you.

Exercise

On the Horse

Your saddle has a tremendous influence on the way your thighs rest on your horse. When the saddle is too small for you; the knee rolls are incorrectly placed; or the seat is too wide (as in some treeless saddles); you will have difficulty getting your thigh to lie flat. When the saddle is too large; the stirrup bars are placed too far forward; or you are riding with a hollowed back; you might tend to grip with your thighs in an attempt to feel secure. Whatever the cause, riding with a *pinched knee* or *turned-out thigh* makes riding more difficult and both positions can inhibit your horse's willingness to go forward (see Susan Harris' description of forward movement on p. 66).

Determining the Correct Seat Size

Your saddle needs to accommodate the length of your thigh as well as the shape of your buttocks. In addition, the saddle's twist needs to match your pelvic shape to free your hips and offer you a comfortable position for your leg. (Note: Not all women need a wide twist!)

When your leg lies flat on your saddle, your weight is distributed around the horse's rib cage through your skeleton (fig. 30.1). This *increased* surface area *decreases* pressure on the horse's back in any one place. Think of a broad firm hug as opposed to being poked in the back.

Providing your saddle fits, when your thigh is flat, the area at the top of the thigh rests—it doesn't grip—along the twist of the seat. The support of the upper thigh protects the front of the pelvis from getting bumped into the pommel. When your knees are turned out there is little to stop you from banging into the front of the saddle, and when the saddle is too small—or the twist is too wide—you may not be able to avoid hitting it.

Also check your stirrup length. Shortening a hole or two can make a world of difference, but it does send you into the back of the saddle so be sure the seat size is big enough. When it isn't, your buttocks will ride up onto the cantle

30.1   A good thigh position. Note its
even contact with the saddle with no
gaps or pinching at the knee.

30.2   Here, the knee is turned out.

30.3   The rider is gripping with her
thigh. Notice how her lower leg is drawn
back, creating a pivot point at the knee.

and cause your pelvis to tip forward and down, creating a hollow back and
putting excessive pressure on the horse under the back of the saddle.

Again, a well-fitting saddle is important for comfort in the pelvic area. If
you are getting hurt there, you need to reevaluate your saddle and how you
are sitting in it. When the thigh correctly lies flat on the saddle, the femur
(thighbone) becomes a structural support for stability without having to brace
your joints. This minimizes the amount of muscular effort needed to properly
adhere to the saddle—and horse.

Riding with your knees *turned out* places most of your weight directly on
the horse's back when sitting on him, and exclusively on the stirrups in rising
trot or in the forward jumping position (fig. 30.2). This position concentrates
pressure on the horse's back in the area of the stirrup bars.

Pinching or gripping with your knees minimizes the surface area over which your weight is distributed, and also takes a lot of muscular effort (fig. 30.3). Pinching limits your ability to follow the horse's motion and can restrict the horse's breathing since you are essentially squeezing his rib cage. Can you imagine what it might be like to have someone constantly gripping your ribs?

If you pinch when jumping, your knee becomes a pivot point. Instead of absorbing the jump with flexible hips, knees, and ankles, you pitch forward, rotating over your knee. This may cause your lower leg to flip backward no matter how much weight you try to put into your heels. A jumping saddle that is too small for you or doesn't fit well in other aspects can also cause the lower leg to swing back.

On your horse (and off, as well) experiment with turning your thigh in from the hip (*internal rotation*), and out (*external rotation*). Notice that you have to let go with your buttocks in order to turn the knee in. Look for the flat of your thigh to rest on the saddle. This widens the back of your seat and reduces the bouncing effect when sitting the trot.

If you find you are still having difficulty achieving this position, check your saddle fit. For more information on saddle fit, I highly recommend *The Pain-Free Back and Saddle Fit Book,* and the DVD, *English Saddles: How to Fit—Pain Free*, both by Joyce Harman DVM, MRCVS and available at www.murdochmethod.com.

31 Better Contact for Riders with Thin Thighs

Training Aids
Two small towels

Use this 5-Minute Fix to improve your thigh contact. If you have thin thighs or ride a slab-sided horse, putting a towel under each saddle flap can make a real difference to your overall comfort and security, especially when jumping. (Note: If you do not have a gap between your thigh and the saddle you can probably skip this lesson.)

Do you:

- Have a hard time finding contact through the upper part of your legs?

- Have thin thighs—as often seen in children and teenagers?

- Tend to grip with your knees or brace against your stirrup to stabilize yourself in the jumping position?

- Ride a very narrow, slab-sided horse?

Here's a quick tip to improve your thigh contact, overall balance, and stability on the flat and over fences.

Notice how your thighs lie on the saddle. Is there a gap under your thigh when your knee is resting on the knee-roll? Can you slide your hand under your thigh (fig. 31.1)? Do you feel like you have to work hard or grip with your knees to maintain your jumping position?

Your thigh is a major part of your seat, especially when jumping in two-point position (see Fix 18, p. 72). When the inner thigh cannot be in contact with the saddle, you lose this important weight-bearing surface area, and you have to shift your weight to your knees or feet. This can cause issues such as your feet falling asleep; gripping with your calves; pinching with your knees; pivoting over them; or falling back in the saddle.

If you ride a wide horse, it is unlikely that you will need this Fix, but you should still check for a gap. Sometimes it is caused by the way the saddle fits your leg, and not the width of your horse. A wide horse generally fills out under your thigh *too* much, causing your knees to turn out so that you grip with the back of the legs. This restricts the movement in your hips and can be uncomfortable (see Fix 29, p. 114). Many people on very wide horses wind up in the chair-seat position (sitting back with their legs out in front of them) because it alleviates tension in the hips. Hip pain is a very real concern and is important to consider when assessing how your horse's shape and weight, and how the saddle, fits you.

31.1 This teenager has long thin legs, and her thigh does not make contact with the saddle.

EXERCISE

On the Horse

For those of you who have thin thighs or are on a narrow, slab-sided horse, this exercise is an easy way to improve your thigh contact. Find two small hand towels. Place a towel underneath each flap of your saddle. Be sure to eliminate the wrinkles and be careful not to have abrupt edges, which might create lumps under your leg. Now mount up and ride (if you have an assistant, she can place the towels with you already in the saddle—figs. 31.2 A–D).

Notice how much support you gain when the gap between the saddle and your thigh is filled in. You can achieve contact with the saddle and the horse without gripping. Take your jumping position and feel how the towels help you feel more secure (see fig. 12.1, p. 52). Filling in the gap distributes your weight through your thighs, increases your stability, and decreases the need to brace against the stirrups. If you are not sure that you like the feeling, take the towels out (this will only take a moment) and ride again. Notice the difference. Experiment to find just the right towel size and thickness.

31.2 A–D Note the hollow area in the thigh area of the saddle (A). This can also be caused by a narrow or thin horse—although not in this case! I take a small hand towel, fold it in half, and place it under the saddle flap (B). The towel fills out the area where the top of the rider's thigh will rest (C). The gap between the rider's thigh and the saddle is gone (D). The rider can use her thigh on the saddle for support without pinching with her knee.

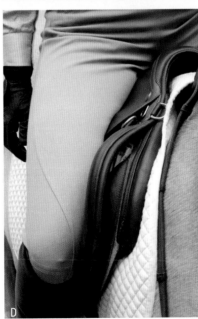

32 Solve Your Leg Position with an Equiband

●●●○○●●

Training Aid
Equiband

Caution
When using the Equiband, it is extremely important to acclimatize the horse to it first. Make sure the horse is not disturbed by the sound or smell of the band and keep the excess material under control while tying the band onto the stirrups.

Stop
If your horse is fearful, snorts, or shows signs of anxiety when you present the Equiband, do not continue the exercise. Instead, do some groundwork to get your horse accustomed to this Training Aid before you put it on your saddle.

Use this 5-Minute Fix to develop a correct leg position. Riding with an Equiband can completely eradicate the habit of pushing the stirrups forward, stabilize your position, and help you find the correct way to get your heels down.

Do you:

- Have trouble keeping your leg underneath you?

- Get pitched forward or fall back when your horse makes a sudden stop or start?

- Have difficulty rising to the trot?

- Brace your feet against the stirrups in order to get your heels down?

- Find your horse has a hollow or sore back?

- Feel as if you are trying as hard as you can, but you still have trouble sitting correctly?

Bracing yourself against the stirrups and/or a saddle with poorly placed stirrup bars may be the cause of your problems.

The classical alignment of ear, shoulder, hip, and ankle is important for all types of riding, including dressage, hunters on the flat, gaited horses, or on the trail. A classical alignment acknowledges and minimizes the influence of gravity and allows you to move with your horse. In this position, you are able to absorb his motion and alleviate excessive pressure on his back. Your legs act like a shock absorbers (flexing at the hips, knees, and ankles) when aligned underneath your body (see Fix 50, p.194).

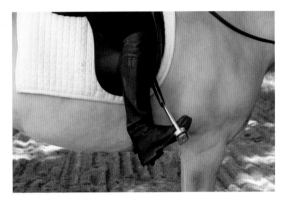

32.1   I am bracing against the stirrup. I have pushed the stirrup forward so that my foot is in front of the horse's elbow. The stirrup leather is at an angle instead of hanging perpendicularly to the ground, which means I am the reason the leather is forward. All of my weight is on the horse's back instead of being distributed between my seat and legs.

Ideally, when your legs are in position (ankle aligned with ear, shoulder, and hip), the stirrup leathers hang straight down toward the ground and remain stable with little to no swing. However, stirrup bars are not always well placed: when too far forward and with the leathers hanging vertically, the rider is put into a chair-seat position. Some riders override this by physically holding their legs back in place, evidenced by stirrup leathers that are angled back from the stirrup bars toward the horse's tail. Unfortunately, the muscular effort involved in holding the stirrups back restricts the rider from using the legs correctly.

Another situation that causes the chair-seat position is when the rider, in an attempt to get her weight into her heels, pushes the stirrups out of alignment (see Fix 12, p. 51, for information on heels down). You can see this because the leathers will angle forward toward the horse's head (fig. 32.1). When you incorrectly apply pressure to the stirrups, they can act like pendulums, swinging forward.

Other riders intentionally sit in a chair seat because it is more comfortable or they believe it makes the horse perform better. In most cases, this riding position makes the horse's job harder, and can cause him back pain because all the rider's weight comes down onto his back instead of being distributed between the seat and legs around the horse.

In addition, when the rider rises or stands in the stirrups from the chair-seat position, all of her weight is transmitted forward *through the stirrup bars* to the horse's back, causing the points of the saddle's tree to dig into the horse's shoulder area. Because her legs are out in front instead of underneath her, the rider typically falls back into the saddle on the "sit phase" of each trot stride instead of being able to support herself on the way down.

Ideally, your weight should be distributed evenly across the entire tree and around the horse's rib cage in order to reduce the pressure on your horse's back. This is accomplished by riding with your legs underneath you as part of your base of support. Once you recognize the value of classical alignment, the question is how do you overcome the habit of bracing against the stirrups or deal with the stirrup bar problem I described earlier without investing in a new saddle?

One answer is supplied with a product I have developed called an Equiband: an inexpensive way to fix saddles with poorly placed stirrup bars and a simple device that acts as "training wheels" for riders who have developed the habit of pushing against the stirrups. The Equiband is made of stretchy material that works like a "V" billet rigging on the saddle. It stabilizes the stirrups to keep them underneath you, yet has enough stretch so that you don't feel restricted as you might if the stirrups were actually tied to the girth.

EXERCISE

On the Ground

To use the Equiband, first acquaint your horse to the sound it makes and its smell. Once he calmly accepts it, tie one end to the *inside* branch of one stirrup (fig. 32.2). Make sure to twist the stirrup leather in the correct direction so it will lie flat against your leg and the stirrup is perpendicular to the horse's

32.2   While off the horse, I tie the Equiband to the stirrups one at a time, using a series of half-hitches along the band to avoid bulk under the ankle. Note that without a rider, this stirrup hangs vertically and is well placed.

32.3   The Equiband is tied securely to the inside branch of the stirrup. Make sure you turn the stirrup into "rider position" to check that you have done this correctly.

32.4   Place the Equiband over the seat of the saddle so that it is not under tension when you get on and off your horse. Otherwise, the band will pull your stirrups back and can make mounting and dismounting difficult.

side (fig. 32.3). (Note: Never ride with the band over your foot or ankle.) Place the rest of the band over the seat of the saddle and go around to the other stirrup. Again, turn the stirrup into the correct position and tie the remaining end of the band to the inside branch. Leave the band across the seat of the saddle until after you've mounted (fig. 32.4).

For safety, always put the Equiband on the saddle when you are on the ground—if you decide you need it while riding, dismount first. Check your knots periodically if you leave it on the saddle between rides because the knots could slip. And be careful when tying the band on the stirrups: If the horse startles with only one side secure, he take off with a large flapping strap chasing him!

Equiband Tension and Adjustment

The tension of the Equiband can be adjusted by tying it a bit shorter, or by using a stronger band—it comes in three different strengths (see p. 131). You want to feel the Equiband is helping you. To compensate for a stirrup bar that is too far forward, make the band a bit shorter in order to pull the stirrups back underneath your hips. The stirrup leather will be angled backward (toward the horse's tail) when the band is stretched over the cantle of the saddle. When the Equiband does what it should, you will feel secure and balanced without having to struggle to keep your leg in position.

When you don't experience a difference, the Equiband could be too loose, or it might not be a strong enough version to override your habit. On the other hand, when the band is too strong, you will feel as if you are fighting it, or your knees may feel a bit uncomfortable (review the Guidelines for Learning, p. xiv).

When the Equiband is properly adjusted to override a stirrup bar problem, you will feel a sense of ease almost immediately, and rising the trot will feel effortless. If the problem has been created by a habit of pushing your heels forward, it may take a bit longer for you to acclimate to your new leg position. However, in the end, you will find that you can ride with less effort and your horse will be more willing to lift his back and go forward.

On the Horse

In the saddle, place your feet in the stirrups. Lift the band off the seat with one hand and even it out, left to right, over the horse's back before stretching it across the cantle (fig. 32.5). This evens the tension on the two sides of the band. Otherwise, one side might be shorter than the other. If it feels like the band is pulling harder on one stirrup, check that the band is even. If after resetting the band, you still feel as if one side is pulling more, you are feeling the unevenness between your two legs.

As you begin to ride with the band notice if you feel like "fighting" it. The point is not to brace against the band but to let it help you find a better leg position (fig. 32.6). Allow your knees to bend until you no longer feel the tug

32.5 Once mounted with my feet in the stirrups, I lift the Equiband off the saddle and even the tension from side to side, then stretch it over the cantle. This puts tension on the band.

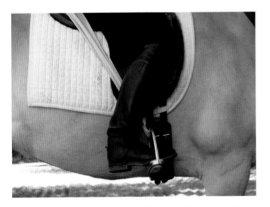

32.6 The Equiband is correcting my bad habit by stabilizing the stirrups and preventing me from pushing them forward.

from the band (see Fix 16, p. 66). Look for a leg position where you don't notice that the band is holding your stirrups back underneath you. Observe what happens to your horse. Generally, horses will go in a better frame with their head down because you are no longer bracing against the stirrups.

Riding with the Equiband for a few weeks can completely retrain your leg position because it eliminates the pendulum action, keeping the stirrup in the correct position underneath you. By using the Equiband, you will discover how to coordinate your hips, knees, and ankles in order to maintain a correct leg position at any stirrup length.

Where to Find the Equiband

Equibands may be purchased through the Murdoch Method online store at www.murdochmethod.com. They come in three different strengths: light, medium, and strong. Strong (gold) is typically for men, medium (silver) is for women and those who have an ingrained habit of pushing the stirrup forward. Light (black) is for children, small women, and those with mild stirrup-bar problems.

To learn how to put an Equiband on your saddle, I recommend my DVD *Ride like a Natural: Part 1— Sitting Right on Your Horse*.

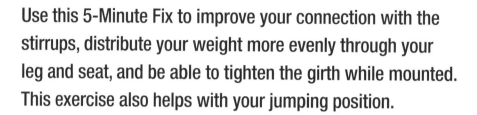

33 | Reach for Your Toes

Use this 5-Minute Fix to improve your connection with the stirrups, distribute your weight more evenly through your leg and seat, and be able to tighten the girth while mounted. This exercise also helps with your jumping position.

> **Do you:**
>
> - Find your feet fall asleep when you ride?
>
> - Feel like you jam against your stirrups?
>
> - Feel unbalanced when you have to open a gates from horseback?
>
> - Feel out of balance in the jumping position?

Here's a quick tip to improve your leg position, "oil" your leg joints, and make it easy for you to tighten the girth while mounted.

Notice how much pressure you have in your stirrups. Could you slip a piece of paper underneath your foot without losing your balance or your stirrup? Do your knees bother you when you ride? Can you easily reach down to tighten your girth from either side? If you have a short girth, can you check it without gripping or worrying about falling off?

If you have long arms, this lesson may be easier for you than for someone with shorter arms. However everyone can do it when you find the right balance. Start slowly and look for gradual improvement. If it is too difficult for you to do in the saddle, practice off the horse while sitting on a flat surface. Then, once you have that mastered, try again in the saddle. Reaching your foot is not the goal. Finding an efficient way to get there is!

EXERCISE

On the Horse

Have an assistant stand at your horse's head the first time you try this so you don't have to worry about the horse moving off as you reach for your foot. Place both reins in one hand and the other hand on your thigh. Leave your feet in the stirrups. Slide your free hand down your thigh, then off the end of your knee in the direction of your foot. Go down and come back up. Do not stay down. Do this several times, but do not push or force. Only go as far as is easy. If you are holding your breath, it isn't easy! Pause for a moment.

Again, slide your hand down your thigh, off your knee, and toward your foot. Is it a bit easier this time? If not, you may need to scoot your buttocks back in the saddle. The key is to get your hips far enough back to counterbalance the weight of your upper body as you lean forward and down toward your foot. When you are too far forward in the saddle, you will have to round or hollow your back to get to your foot.

Rounding causes you to grip with your knee and swing the lower leg back—making it impossible to get to your foot (fig. 33.1). On the other hand, if you hollow your back you won't be able to reach very far down (fig. 33.2). Before you begin again push your pelvis back in the saddle. Be sure to let your knees bend, otherwise you will brace against the stirrup and push yourself out of the saddle (fig. 33.3).

When your back is flat (see Fixes 18 and 19, pp. 72 and 76), it will be much easier to reach your foot (and, of course, the girth too) because you are counterbalancing the weight of your head with your pelvis (fig. 33.4). Once you reach your foot, see if you can pick the foot up just enough to slip a piece of paper underneath. If so, congratulations! You have found where to rest your weight on the saddle without stiffening your leg.

33.1 The rider is too far forward in the saddle. She has rounded her back and cannot reach her foot. She may be able to reach the girth, but it doesn't look easy.

33.2 The rider's back is hollowed, which brings her head up instead of down. Her hand can't get as far as in fig. 33.1.

33.3 The rider has pushed her seat back too far in the saddle. Notice that the angle of her knee has opened and she is bracing against the stirrup.

33.4 The rider has flattened her back, folded at the hips, and is able to reach her toes without falling onto the horse's neck. She can slightly lift her foot out of the stirrup and will have no trouble adjusting her girth.

If you can't pick up your foot it means you still have too much pressure against the stirrup, or worse, you are straightening your knee and bracing against the stirrup. In this position, you could strain your hamstring. Let your knee bend to lift your foot (see Fix 50, p. 194). When you accomplish this lesson on both sides, you will discover that you no longer need to brace against your stirrups.

Mirror, Mirror on the Wall

Use this 5-Minute Fix to improve your overall symmetry and to rehabilitate old injuries. If you have one ankle or hand that is stiff, mirror the other side and see what happens.

Training Aid
Mirror

Do you:

- Have trouble using your right hand as well as your left?

- Have a "dumb" side?

- Feel like your two legs are always quite different?

- Find that every horse you ride goes better in one direction? And it is always the *same* direction?

Here's a quick tip, using a simple mirror, to improve your symmetry.

Next time you ride, notice if one hand or arm is more coordinated than the other. Does one leg rest on the saddle more comfortably? Perhaps you have injured an ankle, and consequently, it lacks flexibility. Or, maybe your pelvis doesn't feel even in the saddle.

Everyone has some degree of asymmetry. As an experiment, look in the mirror and hold a note pad up so that you vertically split the image of your face along your nose (fig. 34.1). Observe how the two halves of your face are different. You might notice that one eye is higher than the other, or that your nose isn't really in the middle of your face. This is perfectly normal; however, asymmetry does affect your balance, and thus your horse.

To improve symmetry, you may have been advised to brush your teeth with your non-dominant hand or muck stalls holding the pitchfork on the opposite side than you would normally. While these techniques will work, you tend not to stick with them because—in the case of stalls, anyway—it takes longer to clean them. Using a mirror, you can trick your brain into thinking that your less capable side is just as handy as the "good" side. You can also improve an old injury or prevent a new injury from causing permanent dysfunction once it heals. I will explain this technique using your legs as the example, but you can do it with any part of your body.

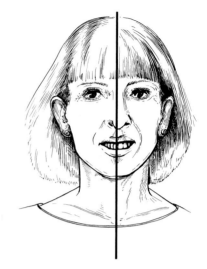

34.1   Look in the mirror and use an object—such as a piece of cardboard or paper—to act as a vertical line to divide your face in half. When comparing the left and right sides, observe how your eyes, nose, mouth, and ears are not symmetrical.

EXERCISE

On the Ground

Walk around the room and determine which leg moves better. In this case, let's say it is your left leg. Find a mirror (a full-length mirror works great) and sit on the floor with the mirror between your legs. Turn the mirror so your left leg is reflected and your right leg is hidden behind the mirror where you can't see it (fig. 34.2).

Start to move your left leg while looking in the mirror. You are now seeing a mirror image. When you move your left leg it seems as though you are seeing your "right leg" in the mirror. Continue moving your left leg until your brain "acknowledges" that this image is your right leg (fig. 34.3). You will know when this happens, believe me! Continue looking in the mirror for a while longer while moving your left leg in as many different ways as you can think up. Then, stand up and go for a walk. Feel the difference in your right leg. It will now feel more like your left leg. Occasionally, remind yourself to "look in the mirror" to maintain the new feeling (fig. 34.4).

Drug-Free Pain Management

The mirror technique developed by Vilayanur S. Ramachandran, MD, PhD, is being used by doctors and in hospitals for pain management and movement rehabilitation. By mirroring the "good" side, the brain gets the idea that the "bad" side is also good. The motor cortex reestablishes the connections to the brain cells allocated to this part of your body. You "see" yourself doing the movement and this redefines that part of your body in your brain. As your brain continues to see and feel your new self-image, pain decreases and movement improves.

This technique is being used for treating "phantom pain" and is 90 percent successful—without the use of drugs. I learned about it while watching a clip on CNN one morning. Then, I attended a workshop with the Australian David Butler, author of the book *Explain Pain*. Butler talks about how our brain perceives pain and how we can move out of pain using our brain. He has devised a three-prong treatment for chronic pain, including the mirror technique.

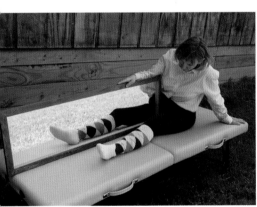

34.2 Sit on the floor with the mirror between your legs. Make the part of your body being reflected as neutral as possible by removing any jewelry that would indicate to your brain which leg you are looking at. Keep the other leg hidden behind the mirror.

34.3 While looking in the mirror move the visible leg around in as many different ways as you can think of until your brain "sees" your other leg in the mirror. Don't worry if the hidden leg starts to move or has sensation.

34.4 No, I don't have three legs! From this angle you can see on both sides of the mirror. But, from where I am looking I can't see the leg behind the mirror. Which leg does your brain think is my right leg?

Wrists and Hands

Introduction

Once your midsection, your arms, and your legs are more stable, you can begin to address your hand position. Most hand problems stem from a faulty seat, which is why the following solutions are not in the beginning of this book. After the underlying cause is resolved many riders still have residual problems because these habits are so ingrained. Also, we are so quick to respond with our hands that it may take something a bit more demanding (like the stick lesson in Fix 40, p. 157) to change these habits.

There are 11 lessons in this section. Although they may seem similar at first, each lesson addresses your hand position from a different perspective. If you find some of the lessons frustrating or difficult, skip them and come back later after you have solidified your overall position by working on the lessons in Section 3 (p. 40). Always keep the Guidelines for Learning (p. xiv) in mind for all these lessons.

35 Your Wrist Connection

Use this 5-Minute Fix as a body-position self-check when approaching a fence, a corner, or turn *before* you use your hands. This simple exercise will improve your overall confidence and balance.

Do you:

- **Have trouble keeping your shoulders back or staying in balance when working on the flat?**

- **Find your horse braces against the reins?**

- **Lose your position on takeoff over a jump?**

- **Use the crest release when you jump—with your hands on the horse's neck—and yet still pitch forward on landing?**

Here's a quick tip to improve your wrist position and overall balance while in the saddle.

Next time you ride, pay attention to your wrists—that area between your hand and your forearm. Do you let your wrists cock inward or round outward? Do you round your shoulders when you round your wrists? In the jumping position, do you cock your wrists and rest them on the horse's neck? Do you feel like your weight is on your hands when using a crest release? Do you have trouble sitting up after a jump? A faulty wrist position can cause serious problems, especially over fences, even when your body is in a good alignment.

Comparable Parts: The Wrist

There are eight bones in your wrist called *carpal* bones. Anatomically, the human wrist is the equivalent of the horse's knee—the *carpus*—on the front leg. The number of bones in the horse's knee can vary between seven and eight. The first carpal bone is not always present. The bones in your wrist allow you to move your hand in many different directions. When riding, you need to stabilize the wrist to help maintain balance in the saddle and a soft contact with the horse's mouth.

35.1 A correct wrist position. Notice the wrists are straight allowing the hands to be in line with the forearms. The sides of the fists rest on the sides of the horse's neck.

35.2 The rider's wrists are cocked inward, thus breaking the line from the hand to the forearm.

35.3 The rider's wrists are rounded outward, breaking the line from the hand to the forearm. Her hands are "punching into" the horse's neck rather than against an imaginary wall in front of her (see Fix 24, p. 94).

Good wrist alignment helps to keep your collarbones wide and open; stabilize your position before, during, and after a fence; and maintain overall balance in the saddle by connecting your hands *through your wrists* to your arms and body (fig. 35.1). Stable wrists clearly transmit the information coming from your seat to the horse's mouth and vice versa.

To find this alignment gently punch your fist into a wall. Meet the wall squarely so that all four knuckles of your fist touch simultaneously. The force of your hand against the wall is transmitted through your wrist into your forearm and body.

Breaking the straight line through the wrist interrupts the flow of information from reins to seat. When the wrists are cocked *inward*, your back tends to hollow and your pelvis tips forward and down, putting you and the horse on the forehand (fig. 35.2).

When the wrists are rounded *outward*, the elbows widen away from the body, your chest drops down, and your shoulders round forward—think of the Incredible Hulk (fig. 35.3). This causes your back to round and your head to drop forward.

And, when your wrists rest on the horse's neck while using a crest release when jumping, you cannot return upright from your hips upon landing (see Fix 19, p. 76). Instead, you have to "throw" your head and chest back to sit up.

When riding in any of these positions, the communication begins and ends at your wrists instead of flowing from your seat via your arms to the bit, and vice versa.

EXERCISE

On the Horse

To find a neutral wrist position, start by closing your hands into soft fists around the reins. Making small movements, cock your wrists *in* then round them *out* (that is, *extend* and *flex* them). Find the middle position between these two movements. Next, break the line of the wrists *downward* (your pinky moves closer to the underside of your forearm) and *upward* (your thumb moves closer to the top of your forearm). Find the middle between these two movements, as well. Finally, locate the midpoint of all four directions. Now, your wrists will be straight and in line with your forearms and hands.

For a crest release, press the finger side of your closed fist against the horse's neck, but keep your wrists off the horse. Imagine softly punching a wall perpendicular to the horse's neck. Press yourself away from the horse's neck to keep back in the saddle over the fence and to sit up on landing.

Two Thumbs Up

Use this 5-Minute Fix as you begin to ask your horse to turn. Rotate your forearm so that your palm is facing *slightly* up and outward. This keeps you from tipping forward and helps you communicate to the horse from your whole body, not just your hands. You may find that, after this exercise, you can turn your horse from your seat.

Do you:

- **Wish you had better hands when riding?**

- **Hear your instructor constantly tell you to make your hands "quiet"?**

- **Find your horse resists when you ask for a turn?**

Here's a quick tip to improve your hand position.

Next time you ride, pay attention to your hands. Notice if they are palms-up, palms-down or somewhere in between. In the sidebar in Fix 20 (p. 82), I talked about the bones of the forearm—the radius and ulna—the upper part of which form the elbow. These two bones also affect hand position.

EXERCISE

On the Ground

Feel the point of your elbow. This is one end of the ulna. Trace the ulna down the side of your forearm where it ends as a bony prominence on the outside of the wrist (see fig. 20.1 A, p. 83). Place your hand on your elbow again. Gently grip your elbow joint, keeping your fingers on the ulna and your thumb in the crease of the elbow joint.

Slowly rotate your forearm by turning your hand so that the palm faces the ceiling and then the floor. You will feel something moving as you turn your hand over. This is the end of the radius as it rotates on the end of the humerus around the ulna. If you move your grip so that the index finger is about halfway between the point of the elbow and the crease (where your thumb is), you might feel the radius moving a bit more clearly. Trace your radius down to the wrist. It ends on the thumb side of the wrist.

Next, extend your arm out in front of you, palm up. Leading with the index finger, bring your finger toward your nose. Go slowly. You will notice that as you touch your nose you have to rotate the forearm; the palm will now be facing toward your nose (figs. 36.1 A & B).

Extend your arm again. This time bend at the elbow *without* rotating the forearm. Keep your palm facing upward

36.1 A & B   With your arm extended, point your index finger (A). In order to touch your nose with your index finger, you must rotate your forearm (B).

36.2   When you bend the elbow without rotating the forearm, your finger ends up pointing over your shoulder.

as you bend your elbow. If you pay attention, instead of touching your nose your index finger will be several inches to the outside of your shoulder (fig. 36.2). Keep the elbow bent and observe the forearm rotation as you bring your index finger toward and away from your nose.

On the Horse

When riding, you want the palms of your hands halfway between the palms-up (facing the sky) position with thumbs facing *away* from each other, and the palms-down (facing the ground) position with thumbs facing *toward* each other (figs. 36.3 A–C). This neutral position, thumbs up, influences the shoulder girdle (see more on this in Fix 9, p. 35). Even when riding with only one hand on the reins, the hand should never be completely flat with the palm down as this position causes your shoulders to round forward.

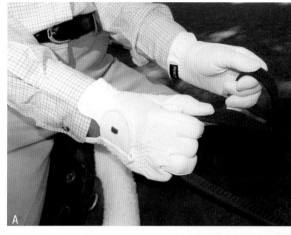

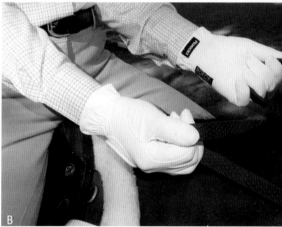

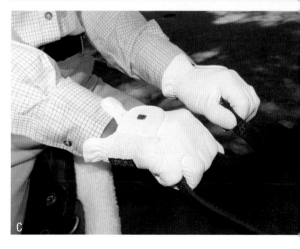

36.3 A–C In A the rider's position is correct with the thumbs up and the hands slightly inward (see Fix 35, p. 140, for information about resting your knuckles on the horse's neck). In B, the hands are turned up too much (the palms are facing the sky), and the rider will try to turn the horse using her upper body instead of her seat. In C, the hands are turned down too much, with the palms facing the ground. The rider will round her shoulders and pull with her arms to turn.

37 Holding Hands

Training Aid
Bridle or piece of string

Use this 5-Minute Fix to improve rein contact. Explore different ways to hold your reins with a human "horse" who can give you feedback. This will help you find better communication.

> **Do you:**
>
> - Find your horse resists your rein aids?
>
> - Feel him hesitate before turning?
>
> - Think you have to "pull your horse around" more than you would like?
>
> - Have sore hands, shoulders, or arms after you ride?
>
> - Think you have "kind hands" but your horse still objects to your contact?

Perhaps what you *think* are soft, kind hands, are not how they *feel* to your horse.

Notice how you hold your reins. Do you grip the reins so much that your knuckles turn white (fig. 37.1)? Or, is your rein contact so "wispy" that it is non-existent? Do you keep the rein between your thumb and forefinger with the other fingers open (fig. 37.2)? Or, does your thumb stick up in the air? Are your biceps soft or hard when you hold the reins? How you hold the reins has a

37.1   This rider has a "death grip" on the reins.

37.2   Riding with open fingers like this can create arm tension, as well as leaving your fingers vulnerable to injury.

direct effect on the contact your horse feels in his mouth.

A closed hand, like a good handshake, gives the most secure feeling to the horse, prevents injury to your fingers, and creates a good connection from your hand to your seat (fig. 37.3).

EXERCISE

On the Ground

To explore your rein contact, find someone to assist you. Take your horse's bridle and have the other person hold the bit. (It is easier to do the exercise when she puts the headstall over her head. Alternatively, she can hold the middle of a long piece of string.)

37.3   Softly closed fingers (pads touching the palms of the hands) protect them from injury, allows the arms and shoulders to stay relaxed, and provides a confident connection from your seat to the bit.

Hold the reins (or ends of string) the way you normally would and have your assistant tell you what the contact feels like. Then change how you are holding the reins: open your fingers; make fists; pinch with your thumb and forefinger;

or hold them only with your ring finger. Finally, hold the reins with a firmly closed hand. Let your helper tell you how each variation feels to her.

Now, ask the assistant to move ahead of you, moving the bit as it would in your horse's mouth at the walk. Can you follow the contact or do you bump the bit repeatedly? Using the reins, ask your assistant to make a turn. Have her tell you what the contact feels like. Then reverse positions and feel what it is like when you are the "horse."

Generally, pinching with the thumb and forefinger causes contraction in your biceps. This feels like pulling to the person playing "horse" at the other end of the reins. "Wispy contact" is not necessarily pleasant either because the "horse" can't tell where the rider is, similar to a wimpy handshake. Holding the reins with your fingers open could leave you with broken fingers if your horse suddenly startled. In contrast, holding the reins so that the pads of your fingers touch the palm of your hand is reassuring to the horse. Rotate your palm slightly *upward* (like turning a key in a lock) to keep the upper arm close to your body. Now, you can turn from your pelvis instead of your shoulders, as long as you don't pull your shoulders up (see Fix 22, p. 88).

On the Horse

Once you have explored rein contact with a person giving you feedback, you will be more aware of your contact when you ride. Experiment with different ways to hold the reins looking for the one that seems to be the most concise, clear way of communicating. You may find that the less muscle you use, the happier your horse will be.

Find Your Finger Strength **38**

Use this 5-Minute Fix to find a good hold on the reins without tensing your shoulders. Finding the connection from your ring finger up the back of your arm allows your biceps to soften while deepening your seat.

Training Aid
Bridle or piece of string

> **Do you:**
>
> • Let your reins slip through your fingers?
>
> • Pinch the reins with your thumb and forefinger thinking this creates a light contact?
>
> • Find your horse pulls you out of the saddle?
>
> • Have trouble maintaining your rein length?
>
> • Tense your shoulders when holding the reins?

Here's a quick tip to help you discover a strong—yet soft—hold on your reins. Many riders hold their reins without considering the effect it has on the horse and their own riding position. Others have arthritic hands that limit how they can hold the reins (see Fix 44, p. 170).

Notice how you hold your reins. Do you press your thumb down hard onto your index finger, flattening your thumb joints (fig. 38.1)? Do you ride with your fingers open? Do you ride with your reins under your pinky finger

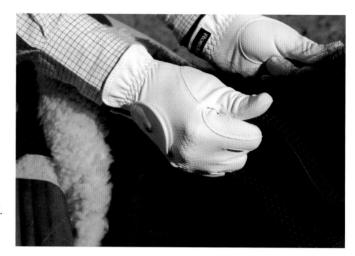

38.1 Pinching the rein with your thumb and forefinger creates tension in the hand and wrist. This tends to shift a rider's balance forward instead of sitting firmly in the saddle.

or between your pinky and ring fingers? While there are many ways to hold the reins, it is important to understand how your fingers relate to your seat through your arms and which method provides the best connection for both you and your horse.

EXERCISE
On the Ground

Pinch a rein or piece of string between your thumb and forefinger. Grasp the other end of the rein and pull—or have a friend do it. Follow the line of action up through your arm and feel which of your arm muscles is activated when you hold the rein with just these two fingers. Do you tense your biceps? Resisting the pull with your biceps creates tension along the front of your body, draws your shoulders up and in toward each other, and tends to pitch you forward out of the saddle.

Now, run the rein around one finger at a time and pull as above. If possible, make a circle with your finger by touching its pad to your palm before pulling on the rein. This prevents the rein from slipping.

Notice that as you move from index to pinky finger, you increasingly feel the pull go from the biceps in the front of your arm to the back of your arm behind the elbow and up through the triceps, especially when using the ring finger. When you activate the triceps through the ring finger, you connect your hand to the back of your body, deepen your elbow toward your pelvis, and sink deeper into the saddle. You may also get this feeling with your pinky, but this finger is not very strong. Therefore, the strongest single-finger connection to your seat is your ring finger. When you feel its strength, you will understand why most riding gloves are reinforced along this finger.

Add more fingers into your hand position. Start by holding the rein around both the ring and middle fingers. Keep the pad of your middle or ring finger softly touching the palm of your hand to prevent the rein from slipping. In the saddle, this will give you a better contact with the horse's mouth.

Pull on the rein with your other hand again and feel how secure this is *without* using your index finger and thumb. Then run the rein from under your ring finger over your index finger. Let the pad of your thumb rest on top of the rein. Keep the thumb slightly bent so that you don't stiffen it, thus creating tension. You will maintain a connection through the ring finger to the triceps if you keep your thumb from pressing down hard on the rein.

If you have arthritic hands, find the finger that is easiest to close. Test each finger to see how much strength you have when you connect the pad of the finger to the palm of your hand. Find the finger that gives you the greatest amount of hand strength for holding the reins. This may not be the same finger for each hand. You need to find out what works best for you and then test this when on the horse.

On the Horse

Experiment with different finger positions on the reins while riding, and watch the horse's response. See if he relaxes into the rein contact or becomes fussy with his mouth. Find out what feels most familiar to you and what becomes the most comfortable for your horse.

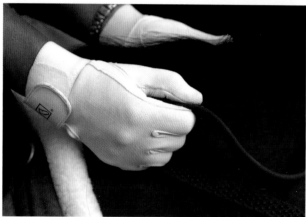

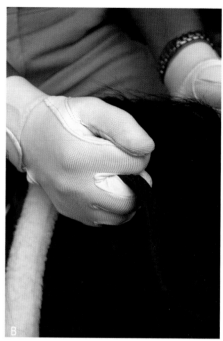

38.2 A & B   Hold the rein so that it is around your ring finger only and close the finger so its pad is touching the palm of your hand (A). Then run the rein under your ring and over your middle finger (B). Be sure to close your hand so the pads of your fingers touch the palm. Feel how you can't pinch the rein in this position.

38.3   Run the rein under your ring finger and over your index finger. Still visualize holding the rein with your ring finger only so that your thumb doesn't press down hard on the index finger. Notice how you can vibrate the rein with your ring finger in order to send a subtle message to your horse's mouth.

What happens when you hold your reins first, with your ring finger only, and second, between your ring and pinky fingers and over your middle finger (figs. 38.2 A & B)? As you ride, feel how you can maintain a good contact holding the rein with only these two fingers. Notice how you can communicate clearly with your seat through the reins. Then, add in your index finger making sure to keep your thumb *softly* resting on top of the rein (fig. 38.3).

Steady Your Bit Contact

Use this 5-Minute Fix to improve your contact to your horse's mouth. When you keep your hands closed on the reins and fixed to the saddle, your reins act like side-reins, steady and consistent. To maintain this hand position you must allow your seat to move in relation to the horse. The horse can learn to accept this fixed rein provided he is moving forward (see Susan Harris' description of forward movement on p. 66).

Training Aid
Chair

Caution
Immediately release your hands if either you or your horse get stressed from your reins being in a fixed position.

Stop
Discontinue the exercise if your horse strongly objects to the fixed rein, especially if he tosses his head repeatedly.

Do you:

- **Have trouble maintaining a steady contact to your horse's mouth?**

- **Find your horse tosses his head or "complains" about your hands?**

- **Find that the harder you try to fix the problem, the worse it gets?**

Here's a quick tip to improve your hand connection and offer your horse a steady contact at the same time.

Many riders worry about having bad hands or being hard on the horse's mouth. Being stiff in the body, or excessively "loose," can both cause you to bump your horse's mouth inadvertently. Avoiding contact altogether by throwing the reins away doesn't solve the problem—it simply hides it. Here's an exercise to help you learn how to have quiet, consistent hands.

Comfort in the Quality of the Contact

Most horses aren't opposed to contact unless they have dental, saddle-fit, or back problems—all of which can appear as a problem in the mouth. In fact, horses often relax when the contact is firm and consistent, and this quality is the mark of a good rider seat.

Notice your rein contact. Do your reins tighten, then slacken repeatedly? Is one rein always shorter than the other? Or, does one rein mysteriously get too long all the time? Do you drop the contact periodically? Do you stiffen during transitions and pull on the reins?

For good hands, you need to keep them essentially "fixed in space," meaning maintained in a specific location, riding your horse *to* your hands with your legs and seat. As your body moves with the horse (see Fix 15, p. 63) your hand position remains unchanged relative to the movement. This keeps you in a good, balanced position. You can refine your rein aids by opening and closing your fingers slightly as a way to invite your horse to yield to the bit, similar to squeezing water out of a sponge.

EXERCISE

On the Ground

Good contact results from the rider and horse being able to move in relation to softly fixed hands. To understand the concept of a fixed hand position, sit in a chair, then stand up and walk around it. Without any restrictions you can move any way you like—there is nothing limiting your relationship to the chair. Now, sit in the chair again, place one hand on it, and stand up and

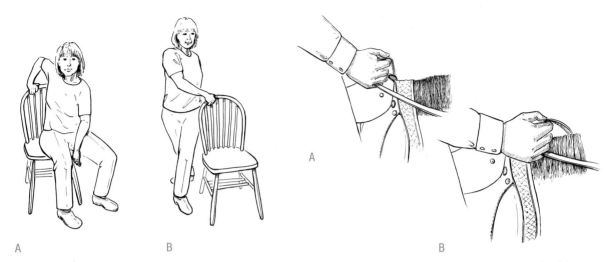

39.1 A & B   While sitting, affix one hand to the back of a chair (A). Leaving your hand in the same place, stand up and walk around your hand (you can let the hand turn). Notice how you move in your hips and legs when your hand is fixed to the chair (B).

39.2 A & B   To "fix your hands" on the saddle, place the pinky finger side of your fist on the pommel (A), or if you have long arms, rest the pinky finger side of your hands in front of the pommel or horse's withers (B).

walk around it without releasing your grip (figs. 39.1 A & B). Your movement changes dramatically. You discover new ways to move your legs and hips that you would not have discovered without fixing your hand to the chair.

On the Horse

To fix your hands while riding, place them on the horse's withers, or on the saddle. Where you rest your hands depends on your arm length (figs. 39.2 A & B). Keep your wrists straight, pressing the pinky fingers of your softly closed fists down against the saddle or horse. You can shorten or lengthen the reins as you need to, then return your hands to this fixed position.

Start to ride at the walk, keeping your hands fixed in place. Let your horse settle into a quiet place as he begins to adjust to your fixed hands. Your length of rein can vary depending on how much control you need and if your horse wants to stretch down through his neck. As you get better at this exercise, you will find that you can ride your horse at any rein length because he will "fill into" the length you offer (if not, see Fix 26, p. 100).

Test out your turning ability. Do you need to lift your hands? Spend some time at the walk until your horse turns from your seat with your hands fixed. When you feel ready, move up to the trot. Do not canter until you feel very confident at the trot.

If your hands will not stay fixed to the horse or saddle, you are not with your horse's movement and/or he is not moving forward—that is, your horse is not in front of your leg and moving into the contact. Check your back and pelvis alignment to be sure that your back is flat and your seat bones are under you (see Fix 10, p. 42).

Keep your hands in place and use your legs to get your horse moving up to the bit. As a "thank you" slightly open your fingers if he makes any attempt to comply until he understands what you want. Once you've corrected your hands and your horse is moving forward, keep them "fixed" near the saddle.

When you have short arms and a long waist, this exercise might be little more difficult. The height of your torso in relation to the length of your upper arms prevents you from placing your hands on the horse's withers or buttons of the saddle with your elbows bent unless you round your back or lean forward. Instead, let your elbow angle open to set your hands. You may no longer have a straight line elbow to bit, but that is fine while practicing this exercise.

.

Excess Stirrup Leather Can Come in Handy

Use this 5-Minute Fix to improve the steadiness of your hands. Holding the stirrup leathers is another way to fix your hands in space. Notice how you have to move yourself toward your hands rather than moving your hands back to you.

Training Aid
Piece of string or Equistrap

Caution
Be careful when holding anything that limits your hand movement. Be sure to let go of the stirrup leathers and/or strap if necessary.

Do you:

- **Have trouble keeping your hands steady?**

- **Find they want to bounce around?**

- **Find your hands move up and down with your body instead of remaining in place when you post the trot?**

Here's another quick tip to help with hand placement.

Notice if your hands remain quiet or move up and down. Do they tend to get uneven with one hand coming back toward your body more than the other? Do you find your instructor always asks you to keep your hands still?

Often riders are unaware their hands are moving. As stated in Fix 39, (p. 153), this is because there is nothing to relate your hands to when they are in position in space over the horse's withers. In order to steady your hands, you need a reference point.

In Fix 39, you started with your hands fixed to the saddle, a very solid connection. Now, in this Fix, your hands are above the saddle but constrained by the stirrup leathers. In the next Fix (Fix 41, p. 160), you will use a strap around the horse's neck to constrain your hands. This is different from what you're about to learn because the strap is coming toward you from the front, more like the reins.

EXERCISE

On the Horse

Take a look at your stirrup leathers. Generally, the end of the stirrup leather is tucked through the loop on the saddle flap to keep it quiet. When the excess leather is long enough, you can use it to steady your hands (fig. 40.1). Grasp the ends of both leathers and bring them forward, holding one in each hand. Holding them *will not* limit sideways hand movement but *will* limit forward and upward movement. Make sure you keep your elbows by your sides and shorten your reins until you have contact with the horse's mouth and the stirrup leathers at the same time.

Avoid Using the "Grab Strap" on Your Saddle

Do not be tempted to use a grab strap that can be attached to the front of the pommel for this exercise. Your hands will end up too close together and too close to your body. Your hands need to be about a shoulder-width apart and in front of you—preferably near the withers.

If your leathers are too short, attach pieces of string to the staple under the skirt on your saddle (fig. 40.2). Cut each piece of string about 8 inches long so you can easily hold them, but so they aren't dangling down around your horse's elbows when you are not using them.

40.1 If your stirrup leathers are long enough, use the ends to steady your hands. Fold each leather forward to minimize the lump under your leg.

40.2 When your leathers aren't long enough, attach a piece of string or strap—about 8 inches long—to the staple under the skirt on your saddle.

Practice letting go of the leathers just in case something happens where you need your hands to be free. Then, ride at all gaits, halt, and turn. Make sure you *pull forward* on the leathers especially when stopping (fig. 40.3). After a while let go of the leathers to see if you can keep your hands quiet without holding on.

40.3 Keep a steady forward pull toward the horse's mouth in order to make the constraint of the leathers effective.

41 Help for Unsteady Hands

●●●●●

Use this 5-Minute Fix to improve your hand position.
I am sure your horse will appreciate your quiet hands
and reward you with his willingness to lower his head
and relax.

Training Aids
Strap or Equistrap,
stick or short whip

Caution
Be careful when holding
the stick, strap, or
both. Your hands are
quite limited by these
training aids; therefore,
it is important that your
horse is quiet and you
are riding in a safe
environment as you
explore this lesson.

Stop
Discontinue the exercise
if your horse becomes
agitated or you feel the
need to use both hands.

> **Do you:**
>
> - **Have trouble keeping your hands steady?**
>
> - **Hear your instructor constantly tell you to keep your hands "quiet"?**
>
> - **Find your hands move up and down as you post?**
>
> - **Tend to drop one hand lower than the other?**

Unsteady hands are a problem for many riders. Here are two suggestions to quickly improve your hand position.

Maintaining steady hands when riding is not easy. The rest of your body needs to move in relation to your hands, which stay in place relative to the horse. In Fix 39 (p. 153), you kept your hands attached to the saddle or the horse. In Fix 40 (p. 157), you used your stirrup leathers to stabilize your hands. Those two lessons got you on your way to obtaining good hands. The next step is being able to take contact by holding your hands in the space above the horse's withers, while keeping them level and steady (fig. 41.1).

Independent Hands

As humans, we are able to move our arms in many ways. We can move our arms in different directions and each arm can move independently of the other. Any time we feel insecure we use our arms by extending them to increase stability and our hands by grasping whatever is closest. Therefore, it is natural for a rider to use her hands to help balance herself. Unfortunately, these hands are usually attached to the reins, and when we use them for support, we are balancing on the horse's mouth.

As a rider's overall balance improves it becomes easier to keep the hands quiet and low regardless of the horse's movement. Excellent riders have what are called "independent hands," meaning they do not need their hands for balance. Their hands remain steady, in a straight line from elbow to bit, even while jumping. To do this, you have to relate to the location of your hands as if they were attached to something, like your hand was on the chair (see figs. 39.1 A & B, p. 155). The rest of your body moves in relation to the fixed point of your hands in space, and that fixed point is generally close to the horse's withers (see Fix 40, p. 157).

EXERCISE

On the Horse

To improve your hand position on your own I have two suggestions:

1 Use an Equistrap or some other type of thin strapping to go around the horse's neck (fig. 41.2) Do not use a closed loop like a jumping strap as this limits the hands too much for this exercise. Hold the strap with your reins, and use your reins as you would normally. Pull upward on the strap (your hands may be above the line of the bit for this exercise). Keep your elbows by your sides. There will be a light tension under the horse's neck. The strap will help to keep your hands in place. Pull upward any time you need to steady yourself (note: only do so if your horse is okay with the idea—check it out first).

The line of action from the strap to your hands is a different angle than the one from the bit to your hands. Providing you keep your elbows down, this increased angle will help you deepen your seat in the saddle when you pull the strap, rather than pulling you forward out of the saddle (see Fix 24, p. 94, for more on sinking deeper into the saddle).

If you habitually pull back on one hand, the other hand will be drawn forward because both hands are holding the strap. This makes the bad habit more obvious so that you consciously recognize it. The strap also stops you from pulling back with both hands at the same time—that is, it will do so as long as you don't let it slip through your fingers. If you let the strap slip, you may well drop one or even both ends, which is why you don't want to tie the ends together. You want to become aware of your habits so you can change them!

2 Ride with a short crop or stick between your hands. Holding your reins normally, place the stick under your thumbs (fig. 41.3). This will help you feel and see when one hand is lower than the other, or closer to your body, since the stick will amplify your hand position (see Fix 27, p. 104).

With one or both of these tools you will learn to sense when your hands are in a good position in space. If you feel awkward and want to "fight" the stick or the strap, it means that your hands are not independent from the rest of your body. It also indicates that this lesson will be of great help to you! (Review Fixes 6, 7, 10, and 12—pp. 22, 27, 42, and 51—to improve your overall stability in order to make this lesson easier.)

Start by using these tools a little each time you ride until you become more comfortable with them. When you no longer notice the Training Aids, switch to using them once a week to check yourself.

You can combine this lesson with Fixes 11, 23, and 32 (pp. 47, 91, and 126), but be sure you have done each lesson individually first! I call the resulting "Combo Fix" my "bondage" lesson because the rider has a variety of constraints all at once. The Equiband and ace bandage keep your arms and legs in place, while the stick and strap fix your hands. In order to follow the horse's movement, you *have* to use your hips!

41.1   A rider with unlevel hands.

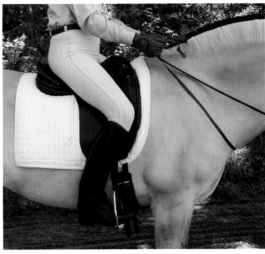

41.2   The rider using the Equistrap. Keep your elbows by your sides while you maintain light tension on the strap. When necessary, pull on the strap (rather than the reins) to help maintain your balance and keep your hands steady.

41.3   The rider using a strap and a stick to help her sense when her hands are in a good position in space. Hold the strap and the reins together under the thumb, and keep the stick on top of the reins.

Bridging the Distance

• • •

Use this 5-Minute Fix when you need greater stability from your reins. Both the full bridge and half bridge rein positions can come in very handy when galloping.

Do you:

- **Gallop your horse on the trail or through open fields?**

- **Want to feel more secure?**

- **Need a free hand to manage a gate?**

Here's a quick tip on how to hold your reins in a full or half bridge, which is useful for many purposes.

The most common way to hold snaffle reins is with one in each hand (fig. 42.1). This method offers you the freedom to move each rein independently. The bight of the reins—the leftover excess rein from your hands to the buckle—typically rests on the horse's shoulder.

Bridging, or "crossing" the reins greatly increases your security and strength. A *full bridge* is obtained by holding reins in both hands (fig. 42.2). When needed, shorten your reins and plant both hands onto the horse's neck so that the horse pulls against himself. This system not only creates a solid, consistent contact but also prevents you from pulling back on the horse's mouth. It is similar to affixing your hands as in Fix 39 (p. 153), only now with the added strength of crossed reins. A full bridge gives you the most

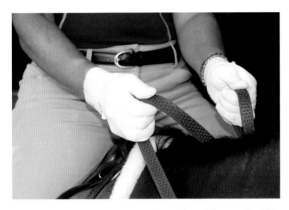

42.1 No bridge—regular use of the reins with a snaffle. This gives you the ability to turn your horse.

42.2 The full bridge offers the greatest amount of stability and strength but little to no turning ability.

"strength" and stability with the least amount of physical effort, which is why it is widely used on the racetrack. It is a very good hand position for getting horses to round up through their top line when galloping. Its disadvantage is that it limits turning ability because you can't move one rein independently.

A *half bridge* is the middle ground between a full bridge and no bridge at all. Both left and right rein are bridged together in one hand, which gives you stability, but you also have flexibility with independent use of your other hand (fig. 42.3). Riders commonly use the half bridge when they want the added strength but also need "steering," for riding a cross-country course, a jumper course, or foxhunting.

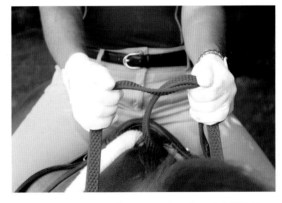

42.3 The half bridge offers more strength and stability than no bridge, but still allows you some turning ability.

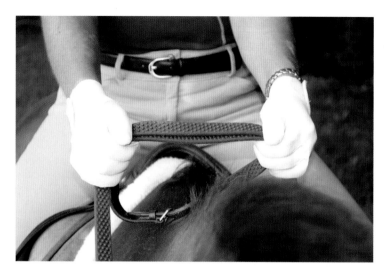

42.4 **Test the bridge for strength: Pull your hands apart while keeping your fingers firmly closed on the reins.**

EXERCISE

On the Horse

To bridge the reins take the bight of the rein from one hand and catch it in the other hand. The two reins will lie on top of each other so that both left and right rein are in each hand. The buckle will fall somewhere between your two hands. Pull your hands apart without letting the reins slide (fig. 42.4). Feel how solid and secure the bridged reins are.

To change from a full bridge to a half bridge, simply let go of the second rein from one hand. For example, take a full bridge; now drop the left rein from your right hand. This gives the right hand freedom to move around. Draw back with your left hand when you want to shorten your right rein. Practice with the other hand.

It is important to practice moving the half bridge back and forth between your two hands. Each hand needs to be able to hold the bridge while the other steers. Once you have become skilled at switching the bridge, the general practice is to hold the half bridge in the outside hand while the inside hand remains free to draw the horse's nose in the direction of the turn.

To go from a half bridge to a full bridge, let go of the loop and reform the bridge between your two hands. Note: This is definitely something better practiced off the horse with a set of reins. Later, you can develop proficiency on the horse at the halt.

Ace Your Contact

This 5-Minute Fix improves your contact and the softness in your horse's neck. Also use it as a test to see how much you are riding with your hands instead of your seat. Make sure to keep your regular reins handy in case they are needed.

Training Aids
Two Ace® bandages

Caution
Be careful when riding with Ace bandages as reins. Keep your regular reins within reach in case you pull one side of the Ace bandages off the bit. Only move up to trot and canter *after* you are sure that your horse will do downward transitions and stop.

Stop
Take up your regular reins if you feel uncomfortable or your horse is getting out of control.

Do you:

- Have trouble getting your horse to take contact with the bit?

- Find it difficult to keep the contact steady?

- Tend to lock your elbows?

- Find your horse simply lets the reins go slack when you give the reins forward instead of stretching downward into the contact?

Here's a quick tip to help you improve your ability to follow your horse's mouth and his ability to accept your contact.

Notice if your horse seems "allergic" to the bit. Does he snatch at it, drop the contact, or fail to stretch down when you offer the reins? Are you afraid to let your horse stretch down? Do you find yourself sawing at your horse's mouth, alternately pulling on each rein, trying to get him to lower his head? Or, do you simply pull on the reins all the time?

Perhaps your horse is simply "dead" to the bit. In order to get your horse to have a "live" feeling in his mouth and stretch toward the bit, you need to offer him an elastic but definite contact. If your horse is stiff in his neck, he needs some help learning how to let go. Here's a simple way to achieve both goals.

Find two fairly new Ace bandages about 2 inches wide—old ones lose their stretch. (Note: If your horse has a short neck you may only need one bandage.) Form a pair of reins by tying the two bandages together. Attach their ends to each side of the bit with a knot. Use a half hitch to find out how much you pull on your horse's mouth—if you pull too much on this knot, you will pull the bandage right off the bit! You can also tie a secure enough knot so the bandages cannot come loose from the bit. You will find out if you pull too much when you attempt to remove them. If the knots are near impossible to undo, you were definitely pulling too much.

EXERCISE

On the Horse

Begin using your regular reins with the Ace bandages loose on your horse's neck (fig. 43.1). You can tie them in a knot if they are in the way. While standing still take up the bandages along with your regular reins, leaving the latter a little slack (figs. 43.2). Make sure you are in an enclosed area because you may not have very much control at first. Using the bandages, ask your horse to turn his head a little left and right so that you can get a sense of how much the bandages stretch.

Ask your horse to walk and primarily use the bandages as your reins—halt, slow down, and change direction. Does your horse ignore you and continue walking where he wants to go as the bandages give? If you need to use your regular reins to help with steering that is okay, but eventually the goal is to use only the bandages (fig. 43.3).

New Ace bandages have a lot of stretch. Therefore, every time you *pull* on your horse's mouth you will feel it instantly because the bandages "give." Once in a while, you may have to shorten up on the bandages until you find the "bottom"—that is, the place where you have a bit more connection with

43.1 The rider uses the regular reins with the Ace-bandage reins resting on the horse's neck.

43.2 The rider uses a combination of the bandages and leather reins.

your horse's mouth—in order to steer for a moment. However, if you find you constantly seek the bottom of the stretch, then you are right back where you started—pulling. Test yourself to see how little you need to do to get your horse to listen.

Check your ability to steer and stop before you try trotting. If you aren't using your seat to turn you might not be able to go where you want (see Fix 3, p. 10). Sometimes, an intermittent signal works best with the Ace reins, like a car blinker. A "dead pull" on a horse that isn't listening is not going to work because the bandage keeps stretching. Notice if your horse doesn't bend correctly anymore. It may be that you have been holding him in the bend with your hands instead of with your seat. If you spend a little time with this exercise you will discover that you and your horse get softer throughout both your bodies (see Fix 6, p. 22). If you are still having trouble, go back to Fix 26 (p. 100), before you attempt to use the Ace bandages again.

43.3 Here the rider rides with the bandages alone.

44 | Fine-Tune Your Rein Aids

Training Aid
Gripmaster®
Equestrian

Use this 5-Minute Fix to improve your rein contact. Closing all your fingers at once improves your overall grip on the reins to prevent them from slipping through your hands. Exercising each finger individually develops fine motor control for more subtle rein aids.

Do you:

- **Tend to grip the reins too tightly?**

- **Always ride with your fingers open?**

- **Have a history of finger injuries that affect their ability to bend?**

- **Find it hard to use each finger individually in order to give your horse a more subtle rein signal?**

Here's a quick tip to improve your finger dexterity and communication with your horse.

Next time you ride, notice what you do with your hands. Are they balled into tight fists, which "bang" on the horse's mouth? Do you tend to pinch the reins with only your thumb and forefinger while leaving the other fingers wide open? Do you have one "intelligent" hand—that is, with fine motor control—while the other is "dumb"? When you can only use one hand well, your horse will hear a "quiet message" on that side of his mouth, but a "hard and stiff" one on the other.

Maybe you didn't realize that you could give your horse subtle rein aids. In order to have good communication you need to be able to "finger" the reins like a musician playing an instrument, giving your horse a subtle vibration with any or all of your fingers.

To develop good use of your hands, I recommend the Gripmaster. Originally designed for musicians, the Gripmaster helps you develop independent movement of each finger without the other fingers necessarily acting. In addition, it can help you develop hand strength when you are rehabilitating an injury; have weak hand muscles; or one very dominant hand. While you don't want to crush the reins, a certain amount of hand strength is necessary to hold onto them so that they don't slide when your horse decides to try to pull you out of the saddle, or when he stumbles.

Although I recommend you use the Gripmaster in order to practice these rein skills, perhaps you can come up with something similar on your own. The task is to develop individual finger strength and the ability to send similar messages to your horse on both sides of his mouth.

EXERCISE

On the Ground

Begin with the Gripmaster in one hand. Make sure your fingers are bent and not flattened on the keys (fig. 44.1). Press each key separately, slowly one at a time without letting your other fingers press down (fig. 44.2). You might find this difficult at first: Your fingers may seem to have a mind of their own and fly off the keys (fig. 44.3). Continue to use the Gripmaster until you can keep all your fingers

44.1 Keep your fingertips slightly bent on the keys of the Gripmaster so you are using the tips of your fingers.

44.2 Press each key down individually without lifting the other fingers.

44.3 What not to do: Here the rider has tried to use the pad of her index finger to push the key down (instead of the tip). The other fingers have lifted off and the thumb has become tense.

on the keys and press each key individually, without excessive tension. Change hands and find out if this is harder—or easier—with your other hand.

On the Horse

Once you have experimented with the Gripmaster off the horse, carry it in a zippered pocket when you are riding. After warming up, and while walking, use the device with one hand to see if you can again press each key individually. Spend a minute or two working on this, and put it away. Now ride again and feel the difference between your two hands. Repeat the process with the Gripmaster in your other hand.

Getting a Gripmaster®

The Gripmaster comes in three different strengths. I find two of them useful: the Extra Light for children and women with very weak hands, and the Light, suitable for average women and men. You can find Gripmasters in a variety of tack shops or on my website www.murdochmethod.com.

Straighten Your Wrists with Popsicle® Sticks

Use this 5-Minute Fix to improve rein contact and maintain a straight wrist position. Remember that you can still use your fingers, elbows, and arms without breaking the line through your wrists. After riding with Popsicle sticks for a while, remove them to see if you can maintain straight wrists.

Do you:

- **Ride with flopped-down wrists?**

- **Cock your wrists in, or round them out, when holding the reins?**

- **Find that contact to your horse's mouth is inconsistent or flimsy?**

- **Find your horse pulls the reins out of your hands or pulls you out of the saddle?**

Training Aids
Popsicle® sticks, tape

Caution
When riding with Popsicle sticks on your wrists, avoid taping them directly over your wrists and adjust the sticks so that they are not jabbing into you.

Stop
Do not wear the Popsicle sticks when riding young or fractious horses. They could limit your responses.

Here's a quick tip to straighten out the kinks, remind you to keep your wrists straight, and improve communication from your seat to the horse's mouth.

Next time you ride, notice what you do with your wrists. Do you round your wrists outward, bringing the knuckles toward each other (fig. 45.1)? As you round your wrists, do you draw your hands in toward your stomach when you ask your horse to halt? Rounding the wrists brings your hands back toward your seat so that you pull back on the reins. It also causes the shoulders to draw together, the sternum and chest to drop, and the upper back to become rounded. Finally, rounding the wrists blocks the movement of your pelvis so that you ride *hand-to-seat* (drawing the hands backward toward your pelvis) instead of *seat-to-hand* (moving your seat forward toward your hands, which keeps your horse's hindquarters engaged).

Perhaps you cock your wrists inward, toward each other with the hands held to the outside of the forearms (fig. 45.2)? Riders with cocked wrists tend to stick their chest out too far and pull their shoulders back too much, thereby hollowing in the back. This wrist position generally puts both the rider and the horse on the forehand causing the horse to hollow his back and raise his head. If you only cock one wrist, it may be caused by a collapse through one side of your rib cage (see Fixes 8 and 9, pp. 31 and 35, for help with this problem).

Cocking the wrists and resting the wrists on the horse's neck when jumping creates a very insecure position because you can't keep your weight back or sit up easily after the fence. Therefore, when jumping especially, it is important to keep your wrists straight (see Fix 35, p. 140).

Some riders break the line through the wrist upward; the pinky side of the hand is toward the horse's mouth (fig. 45.3). This pulls back slightly on the reins. More importantly, it is difficult to yield the hands forward toward the bit in this position. A rider with the line through the wrist broken upward will also have the tendency to hollow in the back.

Pressing down excessively with the thumb may cause the rider to break the line through the wrist downward (fig. 45.4). Often, riders use this position to shorten the reins. However, breaking the line downward creates a backward pull on the reins and causes the rider to round in the back, riding hand-to-seat instead of seat-to-hand.

45.1 Rounded wrists.

45.2 Wrists cocked in.

45.3 Breaking the line through the wrist upward.

45.4 Breaking the line through the wrist downward.

45.5 Flopped down or "puppy dog" wrists or "piano hands."

45.6 Straight wrists allowing for a clear flow of information from the horse's mouth to the rider's seat.

Hands that are flopped down from the wrist (known as "puppy dog wrists" or "piano hands") tend to be heavy on the horse's mouth (fig. 45.5). Very often horses object to this type of hand position by raising their head due to the effect it has on the bit. In this position, the rider is not carrying her hands but resting them on the horse's mouth. When the wrists are flopped down, the arms and shoulders tend to rise, which often makes the rider's seat less secure and effective. (For more help with this, see Fix 36, p. 143.)

When the wrists are straight there is a clear flow of information from the horse's mouth to the rider's seat, and vice versa (fig. 45.6). Instead of the connection stopping at the wrists or causing a backward pull on the reins, a straight wrist essentially eliminates the negative possibilities created by breaking this line. Therefore, it is important to spend time focusing on your wrist position. The wrists may only be a symptom of a larger problem. If you use this Fix to stabilize your wrists, you are more likely to find the root of the problem.

This exercise provides a simple solution to those wayward wrists by giving you a physical reminder of what you are doing. Find some Popsicle sticks at your local crafts supply store (or in your freezer). Make sure the sticks are dry before proceeding. You may want to find someone to help you with the first step, as it is a bit tricky to do by yourself.

EXERCISE

On the Ground

Before you get on your horse, tape two to four sticks around your wrists. Duct tape works well (be careful which type of tape you use, especially when you have a lot of hair on your forearms or sensitive skin). Where you put the sticks is determined by whether you cock or round your wrists, or break the line through the wrist up or down. Every time you try to deviate from the straight wrist alignment, the sticks will serve as a physical reminder by limiting your movement.

To prevent you from cocking or rounding your wrist, place one stick on the front and back. The stick on the inside of your hand crosses the wrist into the palm, while on other side, it "bridges" from the forearm to the back of the hand. Secure the sticks in place by running tape around your forearm and hand.

Note: Do not put tape directly on the wrist. You are not trying to immobilize your wrist with tape, but simply remind yourself when you move the wrist.

If your tendency is to break the line through the wrist up or down, place one stick along the line of the thumb to the wrist and another from the pinky finger to the forearm on the bottom of the wrist (fig. 45.7). Again, be careful not to tape directly over the wrist when you secure the sticks.

If you have both issues, place one stick each on the top and bottom, and one on the front and back of your wrist so that you have a "frame" around it (figs. 45.8 A & B). Tape the sticks to your hand below your wrist and to the forearm above your wrist. Remember, you are not trying to stop the wrists from moving, only to provide yourself with sensory input when you *do* move them.

On the Horse

Once you have attached the sticks, go for a ride. Start at the walk. At first, you may find the sticks distracting because you keep "bumping" into them. As you continue to get feedback from the sticks you might find you feel less restricted. This is because you are beginning to change whatever caused you to deviate from a straight wrist alignment in the first place.

Over time, riding with the Popsicle sticks will completely eliminate your desire to bend your wrists and you will find a new way to communicate through your seat instead of stopping the conversation at your hands.

45.7 Two sticks, one on the thumb and one on the pinky side, remind the rider not to break the line through the wrist up or down.

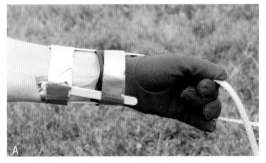

45.8 A & B The four sticks together (here seen from two views) create a frame so that communication from the rider's seat to the horse's mouth is not broken.

Ankles and Feet

Introduction

Ankle mobility is influenced in large part by your hips, whether you jam or rest the foot on the stirrup, and any old ankle injuries. Many of my students start out with stiff ankles but soon realize their ankles are not *causing* the problem; once they learn to lengthen their back and let the weight fall into their heels from their hips, their ankle mobility greatly increases. Your toes can also affect your ankles, knees, and hips, so if you are a habitual "toe cruncher," spend some time learning to spread them out. Go slowly with the lessons on your feet and remember the Guidelines to Learning (p.xiv).

46 | Your Ankle Alignment

Use this 5-Minute Fix to check the alignment of your ankles, which influences your base of support. When the ankles are well aligned, the ankle joints are able to flex allowing your heels to deepen without jamming your feet forward and heels down against the stirrup.

> **Do you:**
>
> - **Have discomfort in your ankles?**
>
> - **Find your feet fall asleep when you ride for long periods of time?**
>
> - **Have trouble getting your heels down?**
>
> - **Push your feet out in front of you?**

All of these common riding problems may be due to your ankle alignment. Your ankles and feet are made up of 26 different bones. I am going to limit this lesson to the ankle area only. In other 5-Minute Fixes, I discuss different parts of your feet (see Fixes 47 and 48, pp. 184 and 189).

Comparable Parts:
The Lower Leg and Ankle

Human

Your lower leg is comprised of two bones: the *tibia* (also known as the shinbone) and the *fibula*. These two bones rest on the *talus*—the ankle bone—which makes up your "true "ankle joint and are responsible for the up-and-down motion of your foot (fig. 46.1 A). The second part of the ankle is the *subtalar* joint where the talus joins the *calcaneus* (the heel bone). The subtalar joint allows side-to-side motion of the foot.

Horse

The equine equivalent to your ankle joint is a portion of the hock. The configuration of the horse's hock is similar when your foot is pointing straight down. The heel bone makes up the point of the hock. The tibia, the large bone in the gaskin between the stifle and the hock, joins the talus—sometimes called the *tibial tarsal bone*. The fibula has faded to a mere sliver of a bone, which ends about halfway down the tibia (fig. 46.1 B). Therefore, in horses, only the tibia joins the talus.

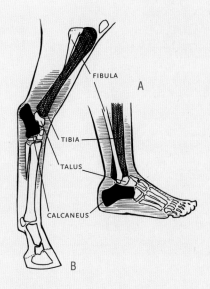

46.1 A & B   The human ankle from the side (A). The horse's hind leg viewed from the side (B). While the proportions are quite different, the bones of the horse's hock are very similar to those of the human ankle.

EXERCISE

On the Ground

Sit in a chair and take your shoes off. Run your hands down the sides of your lower leg. Just before the leg joins the foot you can feel two large bumps, what we often think of as our ankle bones. These bumps, called *malleoli,* are actually the ends of the tibia (on the inside of the leg) and the fibula (on the outside). The tibia and fibula together form an upside-down "U" over the talus, creating the ankle joint (fig. 46.2).

The talus is difficult to feel because it is under and between the malleoli and covered with soft tissue. Imagine where the talus is as you feel the malleoli

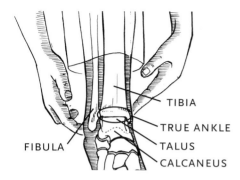

46.2 The malleoli are often what we refer to as the ankle. The lateral malleolus, the lower extremity of the fibula, is on the outside of the ankle, and the medial malleolus from the tibia, is on the inside.

of the tibia and fibula bones. Flex and point your foot to sense the movement in the ankle joint.

Below the talus is the calcaneous, your heel bone (see fig. 46.1 A, p. 181). The talus rests only on the forward portion of the calcaneous, part of which projects backward forming your heel. Take hold of your ankle with one hand on each side below the ends of tibia and fibula and place the other hand on your heel. Move your heel from side to side and up and down. Sense and feel the movement in your ankle joint. You'll have plenty of flexibility to get your heels down when you ride if you can move your true ankle.

Experiment by walking with your ankles cocked in or rolled out. Be careful! You wouldn't want to twist your ankle.

Next time you experience pain in your ankles, numbness in your feet, or feel that your leg position seems insecure, check the alignment of your ankles as I've just described (refer to Fix 29, p. 114, for how to level your feet in the stirrups).

On the Horse

When riding, you want your ankles to be in a similar side-to-side alignment so you don't stress the ankle joints and surrounding ligaments (figs. 46.3 A & B). With your foot in the stirrup, raise and lower your heel. Make small movements. Notice the balance in the ankle and the direction your foot points as you change the height of your heel. When your heel goes above level does your ankle round out? Is the inside of the ankle higher? Does your toe point toward the horse? As your heel goes below level, does it cock inward? Do your toes point away from the horse (toe turning out)? Is the inside of the ankle lower than the outside?

Find the place between the extremes where the ankle is level (parallel to the ground). In this position, your foot may also be parallel to the horse's sides. Feel how your weight is distributed across the ankle. In this position, the true ankle (the one needed to correctly sink your weight into your heels) is available to absorb the horse's movement (figs. 46.4 A–C).

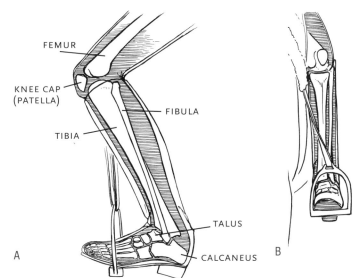

FEMUR

KNEE CAP
(PATELLA)

FIBULA

TIBIA

TALUS

CALCANEUS

A

B

46.3 A & B   View of the foot in the stirrup from the side (A) and the front (B). Think of your foot resting on the ground even though it is in the stirrup. The amount of bend in the ankle and knee is determined by the length of the leather—more open when riding with longer stirrups and more closed when riding with shorter stirrups. The foot, however, remains relatively flat to the ground so that the stirrup remains underneath you.

A   B   C

46.4.A–C   The ankle in A is rounded out and the rider's heel has come up. Notice increased pressure on the pinky toe. In B, the ankle is jammed down and inward, putting a lot of pressure on the inside of the stirrup. It is causing the leather to twist so that the stirrup is no longer perpendicular to the horse's side. The ankle in C is in good alignment. Notice that the foot is weighted evenly from side to side across the stirrup. The ankle is level and there is a sense of depth in the heel without it being jammed down. This ankle will be able to move, absorbing the motion of the horse.

47 | Ankle Gyrations

Training Aid
Roller

Use this 5-Minute Fix to improve your ankle mobility. If you can easily do these ankle movements off the horse, and with your feet out of the stirrups, any stiffness you may have when riding is simply a habit in relation to the stirrup. Remember to occasionally refresh your ankle circles to keep your ankles soft at all times.

> **Do you:**
>
> - Think your ankles feel "stuck"?
>
> - Find they are painful after you ride?
>
> - Have trouble getting your calf "on" your horse?
>
> - Find your pinky toes go numb?
>
> - Try to wrap your legs around your horse but still can't keep them "quiet"?

Here's a way to improve mobility and find a solid, comfortable position for your ankles.

Notice how your foot rests in the stirrup. Do you curl your foot inward? Do you brace your little toe against the outside branch of the stirrup? Is it hard to get your heels down? Do you have contact on the back rather than the inside of your calf? All these problems may be caused by a lack of mobility in the ankle and foot.

Some riders actually have the necessary ankle mobility, but something happens when they pick up the stirrups. The way a rider's foot meets the stirrup seems to be the most ingrained riding habit I come across, and one of the most difficult to change. Perhaps this is because we rely on our feet so much for support. It could be this well-formed habit, not your actual ankle mobility, which is the cause of stiffness and pain.

In order to have a comfortable and solid position in the stirrups, it is essential to have some mobility in the ankles—although probably not as much as you think. There are four primary directions of movement necessary. When working with a rider's ankles and feet, I check to see if she has *side-to-side* movement in the subtalar joint; a *heel-in-and-out* movement, which in part comes from the lower leg and hip (figs. 47.1 A–C); movements called *supination*—an outward roll of the foot—and *pronation*—an inward roll of the foot; and finally, a *heel up-and-down* movement in the true ankle (see sidebar in Fix 46, p. 181).

47.1 A–C While sitting with your big toe resting on the floor, move your heel to the left and right relative to the toe. You will have to swing your calf along with your heel, and there is movement in your knee and hip as you do this, as well. This checks your heel in-and-out movement.

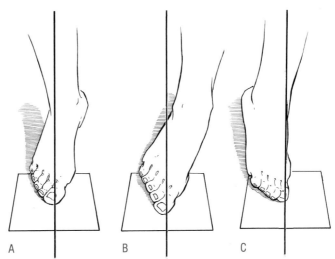

A   B   C

More *Heels Down* Clarification

Why not simply brace down against the stirrup to get your heels down? The answer lies in understanding the names of the muscles involved with moving the foot up and down. In common terminology, bringing the toes upward toward your nose is *dorsiflexion* and when you point your foot downward, it is called *plantarflexion*. Although these movements are both referred to as *flexion*, the muscles associated with them give you a clue about larger movement patterns.

When you point the foot down, you are flexing because the flexor muscles at the back of the leg are doing the work. When you do the opposite and move the top of the foot toward the front of the leg, the extensor muscles are doing the work. While this is called "flexing the ankle," the *extensor muscles* are actually contracting.

Confused? Well most people are, but the bottom line is that when you "flex" your ankle by moving your foot up toward the front of your calf in order to get your heel down, you are using your extensor muscles. Why is this a problem? The knees and lower back sympathetically follow suit and extend, which straightens your legs, hollows your lower back, pushes your buttocks into the back of the saddle, and sends your stirrups forward. Remember, the stirrup is a pendulum (see Fix 14, p. 60).

All this makes you less secure in the saddle because you are unable to absorb the motion of the horse with your primary shock absorbers—hips, knees, and ankles. Therefore, bracing your heels down against the stirrups is counterproductive.

As I pointed out earlier in this book, *heels down* originates from the lower back, not the ankles. When the lower back lengthens, the ligament around the hip joint is no longer under tension, which allows the ball of the hip joint to rotate in the socket (see Fix 19, p. 76). As long as your knee remains softly flexed, the thigh can lengthen downward. Your weight sinks into your heel, which passively closes the angle at the front of the ankle because your foot is resting on the stirrup as if it was the ground. Heels down achieved in this manner gives you a close contact, increases your stability, and allows your joints to absorb the motion of the horse.

Further deepening the heel in dorsiflexion (extending the ankle) makes your calf muscle firm and increases the intensity of your leg aids, providing you *do not push* your foot forward. This should be a momentary event when needed, not a constant effort.

EXERCISE

On the Ground

Start unmounted without boots since they tend to limit ankle mobility. Go gently and don't force anything: When you work on this exercise a little at a time, your ankle mobility will improve. While sitting, place some kind of roller under your foot. You can use a section of a swimming pool "noodle," a can of soup, a rolling pin, or any cylindrical object about 2 inches in diameter (fig. 47.2).

Start with your foot relatively flat on the object, and roll your foot forward and back a little, allowing the ankle to flex and extend. Gradually increase the amount of rolling. Feel how you have to allow the front of the ankle to open. Add lifting and lowering your heel to the rolling with a small move first, then gradually increase the amount. While resting your heel on the roller, extend and flex the ankle without tensing your toes (figs. 47.3 A & B).

Gently rock your ankle side to side with the roller under the ball of your foot, the arch, and the heel (figs. 47.4 A & B). Then, place the ball of your foot on the roller with your heel slightly lifted and swing your elevated heel left and right like you did with your big toe resting on the floor (see figs. 47.1 A–C, p. 185). Again, place your heel on the roller and move the sole of your foot toward and away from you—supination and pronation (figs. 47.5 A & B).

Make circles with your foot when the roller is either under the ball or heel, or as you roll the foot forward and back.

On the Horse

Once you have succeeded at doing all of these movements off the horse, you can do modified versions in the saddle. Take your foot out of the stirrup and perform the ankle circles as if the roller were under your heel. Place your foot in the stirrup and, using the stirrup for support under the ball of your foot, make a vertical circle with your heel. Then allow your foot to rest in the stirrup.

If, while riding, your ankles get painful or stiff, stop, check your lower back and repeat the ankle circles (see Fix 12, p. 51). With your foot in the stirrup, see if you can allow a very small, "soft" circle to happen when you are walking, trotting, and cantering.

47.2 Use a cylindrical object to play with the movement in your ankle. It is a good idea to keep the roller handy so you can supple your ankles while watching television or reading.

47.3 A & B Flex and extend your foot while your heel rests on the roller.

47.4 A & B With the roller under your arch, make small, gentle side-to-side movements from the ankle.

47.5 A & B Resting your heel on the roller, pronate and supinate your foot. Notice how this motion involves the area of the mid foot in order to turn the sole away from you (pinky-toe side is lifted) and toward you (big-toe side is lifted).

Uncovering the Secrets of Your Feet

48
●●

Use this 5-Minute Fix to improve foot comfort and your stability in the saddle. Make sure you have shoes that give your toes enough room to spread out. Your toes will gradually respond to this encouragement, which will improve your foot comfort both on the ground and in the saddle.

Do you:

- Curl your toes inside your boots?

- Jam your big toe up against the top of your boot?

- Feel as if, at any moment, your feet might slip out of your stirrups?

- Find your feet hurt when you get off your horse?

Here's a quick tip to help your feet feel better even when they are already relaxed in the stirrups.

Next time you ride, notice what you do when your feet are inside your boots. Are your toes lying flat on the boot's foot bed? Or, are they pressed

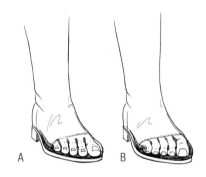

48.1 A & B   Toes in normal position (A) and curled up in the rider's boot (B).

against the top of the boot, or curled up or down (figs. 48.1 A & B). Are you gripping with your toes? Do your toes tend to stiffen when you jump or attempt a difficult movement? How about when you watch someone else jump? Do you wear the correct width shoes so your toes can spread out in the toe box? While it is not possible to see what is happening inside a rider's boot, it is surprising to hear how many people do funny things with their toes when they ride.

Relaxed toes are essential for proper foot function in the stirrup: ankles relaxed and weight sinking down through the heels. When your toes are crunched, you have less foot to support you; it is easier for your foot to slip out of the stirrup; and you are much more unstable. Ill-fitting boots can create foot problems. Footwear should fit comfortably—with the type of socks you want to wear—so you can use your feet efficiently in the stirrups.

Once you have resolved any footwear issues, it is time to address the habits you "hold" in your feet. Feet are extremely opinionated! I can place a rider's leg in beautiful soft alignment, but the moment I even think about putting her foot back in the stirrup, all the old patterns return. Therefore, once you do the following exercise, it is important to keep your toes soft when you pick up your stirrups.

EXERCISE

On the Ground

Start off the horse, without shoes or socks. Take your fingers and gently spread your toes apart. Be very gentle, as some feet are so contracted that even small movements can be painful. Carefully divide your toes and trace the sides of each toe with your index finger down to the base, spreading them gently as you go (fig. 48.2). If this is not painful, interweave your fingers between your toes from the bottom of the foot so your fingers stick up over the toenails (fig. 48.3). Move your toes with your fingers. Then, interlace your fingers from the topside so their tips point toward the sole of the foot. Find out how much

48.2 Trace the inside edges of each toe with your index finger. Go gently as initially this can be painful if your toes are really contracted.

48.3 Interlace your fingers with your toes from underneath.

48.4 Spread your toes out in your boots, giving each toe sufficient room.

you are able to move your toes. If you really want a challenge, interweave the toes of your two feet together!

Separate your hands from your feet and stand up. What do your feet feel like to stand on? How large are they? How much surface area do they cover? Walk around for a moment before you put on your boots, then continue to walk, remembering the feeling of your toes spread widely apart.

On the Horse

If you are doing this lesson at the barn, mount up and notice if your toes are still spread. Recall the feeling of walking after your toe explorations. Imagine the toes are wide apart or that you have webbed feet like a duck (fig. 48.4). Notice how much more of the stirrup you can feel under your boot. As you ride, remind yourself to let your toes spread out and feel how your hips, knees, and ankles become more supple.

49 Weighing-in on Your Ankles

●●●●●●

Use this 5-Minute Fix to improve your heel position. By using ankle weights, you can learn how to "let go" for a deep heel position without struggling to force your heels down.

Training Aids
Ankle weights, wire ties

Caution
When first using ankle weights, your leg aids may feel heavy and confuse your horse.

Stop
If your horse becomes anxious about the weights touching his sides, dismount immediately.

In Fix 12 (p. 51), I gave you an exercise to help you feel the connection from your lower back to your heels. In order for the weight to fall through the heels, the lower back has to be flattened. However, even when the back is correct, some riders still can't find this "deep" feeling—due to injury, old habits, or just not being sure of what to look for (fig. 49.1). Here's a quick tip to give your ankles the reminder they need to allow your weight to fall through your heels.

Look through your old gym equipment and see if you have a pair of ankle weights. A 1- or 2- pound weight is all you need. You may want to add a Velcro strip to the existing strap or some wire ties to make it long enough to fit around your boot (fig. 49.2).

EXERCISE

On the Horse

Strap the ankle weights around your boots, not in the typical fashion but in a way so that the weight hangs below your heel (fig. 49.3). If you find it tricky to get on your horse with the weights in place, have an assistant put them on your boots after you've mounted.

Take a moment at the halt to let your horse get used to the feeling of the weights on his sides. They might feel bulky or touch his sides in a different place than your leg normally does. Give yourself a minute to let the ankle weights draw your heels down and back, anchoring your legs. Do not tense your legs or resist the weights. Instead, "let things sink."

Begin to ride at the walk. If your horse is a bit concerned about the contact, stop and gently rub the weights on his sides for a moment. It may be more leg pressure than he is used to. Even though your leg aids might feel a bit different, most horses generally acclimate to the weights in a few minutes.

Once your horse is okay, continue with your ride as usual. You might even forget that the weights are there, but you will notice an added level of security in your overall position and depth of heel. You may want to ride with the weights for a week or so to develop a new habit. Then ride without the weights and see if you can recreate the deep feeling you had with them on. Put the weights back on whenever you need a reminder to let go and deepen your heels.

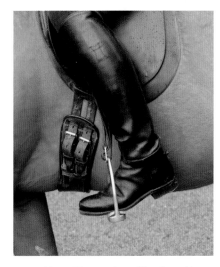

49.1 Many riders tend to stiffen the ankles or brace on their toes, thereby preventing their weight from sinking through the heels.

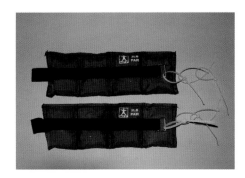

49.2 A simple pair of ankle weights, perhaps with added Velcro or wire ties to reach around your boots, can help give the rider a sense of "weighting" the ankle.

49.3 Place the ankle weight around the boot so it hangs down off the heel a bit. This will remind you to "let go" in the ankle so your heel can sink down.

50 Find the Balance Point of Your Foot

●●●○

Caution
Be careful when first
tapping on the bottom of
the rider's foot—it could
frighten the horse.

Use this 5-Minute Fix to help you find the balance point of your foot. When you rest on it, you will have more flexibility in your hip, knee, and ankle joints, and your foot will be more secure in the stirrup.

> **Do you:**
>
> - **Find your feet feel tense in the stirrups?**
>
> - **Think the joints in your legs feel stiff?**
>
> - **Frequently lose a stirrup?**
>
> - **Feel out of balance?**

Here's a quick tip to find the stirrup position that gives you the greatest amount of overall stability and, at the same time, flexibility in the hip, knee, and ankle joints.

Notice how you place each foot in the stirrup. Do you jam your pinky toe against the outside branch (fig. 50.1)? Is the stirrup angled across your foot? Do you tend to have just the tips of your toes on the stirrup tread? Do your hips, knees, and ankles feel inflexible? Are your heels braced down against the stirrups?

Many people purchase hinged stirrups in order to ease pain in the knees. It may be, however, that this stiffness results from your placement of the feet on the stirrups, and with a simple adjustment, you can ease the discomfort without a costly investment.

EXERCISE

On the Horse

Find an assistant to help you feel the effects of placing your foot differently on the stirrup. Start by having your toes resting on it. Ask the helper to

50.1   Many people ride with the stirrup too far forward toward the toes and jam their pinky toe against the outside branch of the stirrup.

place her hands under the stirrup and test whether she can easily lift up the stirrup (fig. 50.2). Notice how difficult this is for you: Are your joints flexing easily, or are they instead braced against the stirrup?

Place your foot deeper into the stirrup so that the ball of your foot rests on the stirrup tread. Again, have your assistant attempt to lift the stirrup (fig. 50.3). Look for movement in your joints and see how easily your helper is able to lift the stirrup with your foot on it. Put the stirrup behind the ball of your foot and repeat the stirrup-lifting test (fig. 50.4).

Take your foot out of the stirrup and have the assistant tap on the sole of your boot using the palm of her hand. (This may be a bit hard on her hand so you might want to return the favor when she is in the saddle.) Have her start at the toe and work back toward the arch of the boot (figs. 50.5 A–C). Listen to the sound made by the tapping. It will sound hollow when you are at the part of your foot that belongs on the stirrup—just behind the ball of the foot. This place is known as the *balance point of the foot*.

Ride with the foot more or less through the stirrup to complete the feeling of having your different parts of your sole rest on the stirrup. Compare movement in your hip, knee, and ankle joints to what you experienced when you

50.2 Have an assistant try to lift the stirrup with only your toes resting on it.

50.3 Try with the stirrup under the balance point of your foot.

50.4 Again, have a helper try to lift the stirrup, this time with the foot too deep in the stirrup.

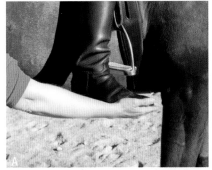

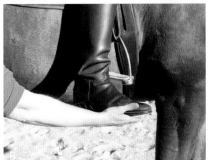

50.5 A–C   Have your assistant tap the sole of your boot in different places to listen for the hollow sound that identifies the balance point of the foot: toward the toes (A); under the balance point of the foot (B); and under the arch (C).

did the other experiments. Then, place your foot in your old riding position. Notice the difference.

The ideal position for the foot on the stirrup is just behind the ball, the balance point of the foot (fig. 50.6). However, as I've said before, I find that most riders have very "opinionated" feet. This is why it is important to perform the two tests described here to convince you there might be a better place for your foot. Go back and forth several times between the old place and the new place really feeling for differences rather than simply deciding "it doesn't feel right." You might find with a little practice that the new place is better than you initially thought.

50.6   Ride with your foot on the balance point and see how this differs from your usual position.

RESOURCES

Training Aids for the Rider

(As used in all 50 5-Minute Fixes. Some of these items are available at www.wendymurdoch.com/shop.)

- Equistrap or other nylon strap about 80 inches long
- Dowel or stick (about 12 to 15 inches long)
- Two elastic bandages (such as Ace® bandages)
- Washcloth or small towel
- Equiband (three different strengths available)
- Exercise ball
- Dressage whip with lead tape (available through a golfer supply store) or washers
- Vetrap®
- Plumb bob (a nut on a string works just fine)
- Cardboard or shims for stirrups
- Eye patch
- Short elastic band for attaching to post
- Gripmaster®
- Popsicle® sticks
- Belted pouch or pack and saddle-pad weights (rice also works for weights)
- Ankle weights with wire ties
- Pool noodle or small foam roller for feet
- Full-length mirror
- Tilt board
- Gardener's kneeling pad

Recommended Reading and Viewing

Simplify Your Riding (book) and *Ride Like a Natural*® *Parts 1–3* (DVDs) by Wendy Murdoch (www.murdochmethod.com)

The Pain-Free Back and *Saddle Fit Book* and *English Saddles: How to Fit— Pain-Free* DVD by Dr. Joyce Harman (www.harmanyequine.com)

Centered Riding by Sally Swift (www.centeredriding.org)

Bones for Life® (www.bonesforlife.com)

The Feldenkrais® Method (www.feldenkrais.com)

The Tellington Method (www.ttouch.com)

MBS Academy—Mind Body Study (www.mbsacademy.org)

Contact Information

Send your suggestions ideas for other 5-Minute Fixes to Wendy Murdoch—visit her contact page at www.murdochmethod.com.

INDEX